EVOLVED

With love to my mum and dad, Andrea and Phil, and to my daughters, Phoebe and Zoe. You inspire me every day.

DARCEY BUSSELL
EVOLVED

hardie grant books

Pointe Shoes
1989

_____

Photo by Bill Cooper/ArenaPal

FOREWORD

In 1990, for my Autumn/Winter womenswear collection the clothes I designed were inspired by the ballet. Not the jewel-encrusted tutus or the glamorous side of dance costume, but clothes that dancers use to practice and rehearse in, clothes to wear, move and live in and which celebrate the graceful freedom of movement.

For this collection, rather than show the clothes in the traditional format of a fashion show we decided to produce – and this was then a rather new concept – a short film instead, which would be shown at London Fashion Week. For this we obviously needed an exquisitely beautiful dancer to model the clothes, and it was a no-brainer: there was only one on our list and that was the marvellous 20-year old, up-and-coming star of The Royal Ballet, Darcey Bussell. She had just joined the Company to work with the legendary choreographer Kenneth MacMillan on a new production of his ballet *The Prince of the Pagodas*, she had the grace of Margot Fonteyn, the bravura of Rudolph Nureyev and the face of a supermodel. We were smitten with Darcey, *but* could we get the 'powers that be' at The Royal Ballet to release her and *then* get Darcey's agreement to work on our project? Classical ballet is a world of formal, rigid discipline and rules that simply cannot be broken, and what we were proposing would break nearly every rule in the book. Luckily for us, Darcey was keen on the idea of dancing and choreographing a piece to the music of Snap! a dynamic and highly energetic track called 'The Power' from their album *World Power*. Miraculously, The Royal Ballet agreed to let her work with us.

Filming with her was terrific fun, although I suspect less so for Darcey, as she threw herself across the set again and again, using various forms of classical ballet but in an excitingly new and fresh way. I was ecstatic with the results and the film was shown on Friday 9th March 1990, by which time Darcey and I were firm friends. Later, I was very happy indeed when David Bintley, then resident choreographer at The Royal Ballet, asked me to make Darcey's costume for his production of *Tombeaux*, for a charity gala at The Royal Opera House, Covent Garden on the 3rd November 1991, performed in the presence of HRH The Princess of Wales. This changed my life in a wonderful and highly creative way and I continued to work with David Bintley over the next 14 years on several further ballets, mainly for Birmingham Royal Ballet.

So here we are some years on, both our lives have evolved. Darcey is now a Dame of the British Empire, in recognition of a hugely varied and successful career both behind and in front of her. She is still exquisitely beautiful (the result, no doubt, of a blameless life!) and still thinking creatively about all she brings to her continuing work. We have continued to work together on various different projects, and on several occasions I have been able to dress her off-stage as well. I like to think that we have a similar approach to our professional lives, both of us recognising that we can use our talents and abilities in different ways, inspired and guided by our original craft but not hemmed in by it. This passion for extending and enjoying all the possibilities of dance, embodied in this new book, continues to lie at the heart of Darcey's personal and professional evolution.

JASPER CONRAN

The *Azura* P&O Cruise ship
APRIL 2010

On the bridge of the MS *Azura* wearing a dress by Jasper Conran.

Photo © P&O Cruises

INTRODUCTION

I have always enjoyed working with others, been willing to experiment and share ideas to try to create something different and special artistically. I love being exposed to other people's talent and skill. Whilst not premeditated, but evolving naturally, these collaborations have been hugely rewarding in my career as a dancer and beyond. Of course, they didn't always produce what I first visualised, but overall I have been very fortunate and it has allowed me to share my love of dance widely.

It's probably true to say that when I went to The Royal Ballet School aged 13, I had no idea where a career in dancing could possibly take me. Looking back I can see that my life evolved from that love of dance I had as a child. Everything that followed stemmed from that opportunity to be schooled in dance and also that I was prepared to work really hard at it. I just wanted to dance and succeed in impressing my teachers. I suppose I am a good example of someone who thrived in the environment of a regimented and disciplined vocational school.

As a late starter, I had to work hard to catch up with my peers, so when I left The Royal Ballet School and was offered a job in the Sadler's Wells Royal Ballet touring company, I was delighted. Now a working dancer, I discovered that this afforded me more opportunities to explore roles than would be possible in the *corps de ballet* of the main Company. From there, I had the wonderful opportunity to join The Royal Ballet a year later, working with Kenneth MacMillan to dance the lead role in his new production *The Prince of the Pagodas*. Aged just 19, I knew this was an extraordinary opportunity and I also realised, probably for the first time, that I could possibly have a long-term career as a ballet dancer.

As it turned out, my career evolved through dance and beyond, while still encompassing it. My arrival at The Royal Ballet coincided with a new sense that ballet had to be more accessible to survive, to be less of an elite art form, but instead one that everyone could enjoy. I was very keen to promote this and create awareness that dance is an important art form. So initially I became known outside the ballet world, while still representing it, through early poster campaigns and then, later, modelling and photographic shoots. These projects ranged from working with designers like Jasper Conran to campaigns to promote 1940s fashion at the Imperial War Museum, and working with many celebrated photographers like Lord Anthony Snowdon, John Swannell, Anthony Crickmay, Annie Leibovitz and Arthur Elgort. So I had a taste of the commercial world outside ballet whilst I was a dancer; I enjoyed breaking the mould a little while still being dedicated and passionate about my art. I wanted people to know how real we were as dancers.

I couldn't have been happier being a Principal dancer for almost 20 years. I decided to retire at 38 because I felt that I was still in peak form, that I could dance any classical role without having to drop any of the technically demanding parts, but I also wanted to be with my two young daughters, then aged three and six. For a woman, having a natural career break to have children also requires some evolution, resetting and readjustment but I also knew how much I enjoyed working and wanted to continue. What I will always treasure, though, was having the four or five quieter years in Sydney with my husband and the girls while they were young.

I never thought specifically about 'what next' after I retired from The Royal Ballet in 2007. I knew there were things I wanted to explore and naively and optimistically hoped something would turn up! Since returning to the UK and more full-time work, I have been very lucky to have made television documentaries about dance, contributed to dance and health related charities, created a live show *Viva la Diva* with Katherine Jenkins, jumped off an Olympic stadium roof (in a harness!), presented The Royal Ballet cinema relays and now I'm probably best known as a judge on BBC1's *Strictly Come Dancing* television show.

As you might have gathered, I am completely passionate about everyone dancing. Whether you participate in some form of dance or just love to watch it at the theatre or on Saturday night television, dance in all its forms, really *is* for anyone of any ability. We *can* all dance; we *should* all dance. Take up ballet, jazz, hip hop, tap, flamenco, jive, dance fitness – or simply dance to the radio in your kitchen – because moving to music will benefit you throughout your life. I am always going to be a dancer, however old and creaky I become.

I believe that in life, if you are fearless and curious, allowing your ideas to evolve beyond their immediate boundaries, I think they can take you anywhere. This is why I think creative arts like dance must always have a place in education, so that children and young people can benefit from the many attributes they provide. Increasingly, complex societies rely on the creative individual, so let's make sure we always encourage creativity.

I hope this book conveys some of the possibilities that can evolve from creative collaboration and shows my deep and enduring appreciation of the talented artists I have been so fortunate to have worked with.

DARCEY x

I believe that in life, if you are fearless and curious, allowing your ideas to evolve beyond their immediate boundaries, I think they can take you anywhere.

Tryst
MAY 2002

Rehearsing Chistopher Wheeldon's
Tryst with Jonathan Cope.

Photo by Asya Verzhbinsky/Alamy

1

FOUNDATIONS

ELITE SYNCOPATIONS

THE PRINCE OF THE PAGODAS

REHEARSING SWAN LAKE
with Sir Anthony Dowell

THE SLEEPING BEAUTY
with Dame Ninette de Valois

Lord Anthony Snowdon
1986

This was my first ever publicity shot, which
was done for Marks & Spencer while I was still
a student at The Royal Ballet School. I remember
feeling incredibly apprehensive and fearful of what
it would be like to be shot by such a renowned figure
in the photography world. I was so inexperienced
as a muse for a photographer at the time, that my
nerves were clearly evident – it was difficult not to
grip the chair too tightly and appear relaxed. The
photo was part of a campaign of young artists from
different art forms. The image was then used as
a piece of advertising in the programme for the
premiere of *The Prince of the Pagodas* in 1989.

———

*Photo by Lord Anthony Snowdon/courtesy of the
Darcey Bussell Collection*

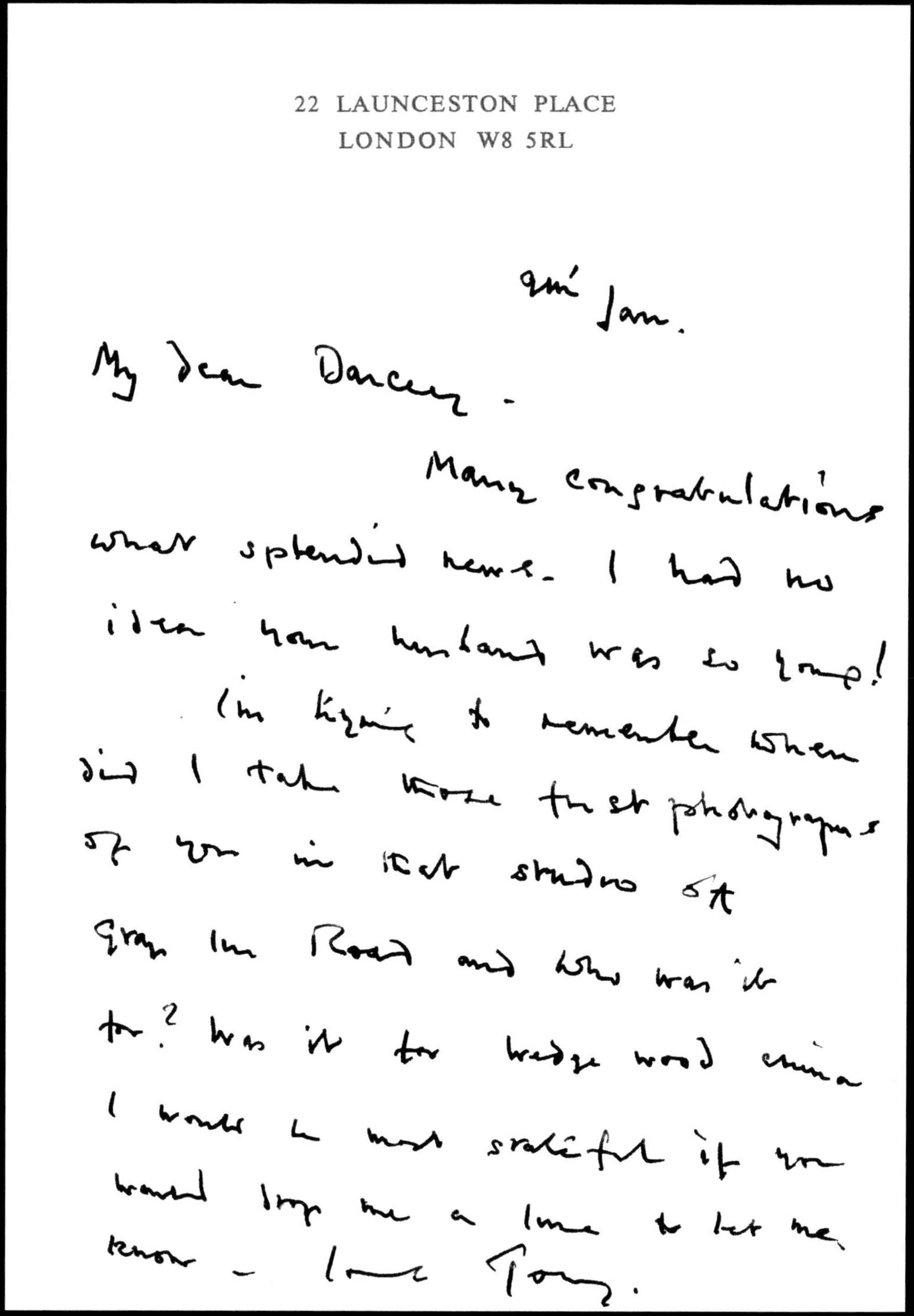

22 LAUNCESTON PLACE
LONDON W8 5RL

9th Jan.

My dear Darcey –

Many congratulations
what splendid news. I had no
idea your husband was so young!

I'm trying to remember when
did I take those first photographs
of you in that studio at
Grays Inn Road and who was it
for? Was it for Wedgewood china
I would be most grateful if you
would drop me a line to let me
know – love Tony.

Sadler's Wells Royal Ballet
1988

First Principal role with Stephen Wicks.

———

Photo © Leslie E. Spatt

ELITE SYNCOPATIONS

Sir Kenneth MacMillan's one-act ballet *Elite Syncopations* is very special for me because it was my first Principal role with Sadler's Wells Royal Ballet when I was only 18. I danced the role of Stop Time Rag girl, created on Dame Merle Park. When I was cast, I didn't know it was the main role in the ballet, which was such a huge honour and my first major opportunity outside the *corps de ballet*. Because I managed to misunderstand the casting – I thought they'd got it wrong and that this wasn't actually my role – very embarrassingly I didn't turn up for the first rehearsal! But I was forgiven and it is one of my favourite roles, for its quirkiness, style and sex appeal.

MacMillan created the ballet in 1974 using ragtime music, including that by Scott Joplin, and the most extraordinary costumes designed by Ian Spurling, which continue to be used today. I remember going for my first costume fitting to discover I'd be wearing this outrageous white Lycra one-piece, with a star on each buttock and one on my… well you can see where on page 19, a bolero-styled jacket dotted with huge pearls and a great top hat that was quite heavy. Given the amount of partnering in this ballet, I was a bit concerned that the giant pearls would be a problem, digging into me every time I was lifted.

The stage is empty apart from a 12-piece orchestra and ragtime jazz pianist, like a jazz club or 1920s speakeasy. They are all in costume too, and there's a huge sense of fun that runs through the whole piece that comes from the characters of the dancers and the fast-paced, gracefully athletic dancing. There's quite a long *pas de deux*, and it starts really subtly. It's deceptive because, at first, the legs aren't too high, the turns not too flashy, but it builds and builds to this precisely timed, syncopated rhythm that's like a very cheeky conversation between the two of us. As we dance, the rest of the cast are on stage, watching, like you might watch the professional dancers in a club, before joining in. The strength of the characters is one of the things that makes the ballet, and the characters are enhanced by Kenneth's innovative choreography and such clever and simple staging.

My first partner for this when I was 19 was Stephen Wicks (who's still a great friend and now runs a glorious florists in Covent Garden). His role demands real attitude, which you can see here, having the arrogance of a suave spiv and the cockiness that he knows he's the leader of the pack. My role is to dance in relationship to that, to answer it in equal measure and be part of the necessary, subtle confidence of the whole ballet.

We performed *Elite Syncopations* everywhere and one of my favourite places was in Japan. It's so unlike the classical work that The Royal Ballet is so renowned for, I don't think the audience there had seen anything like it. It's very strong in its references to the American Jazz Era, which comes across so well, but culturally it's a long way from Japan. But they loved its fun attitude, the syncopated rhythms, the choreography and those costumes!

Japanese Tour of *Elite Syncopations*
17TH FEBRUARY 1993

The photograph on the right was shot by the great Anthony Crickmay for *ES Magazine*. I'm shown with Zoltán Solymosi during his first year with the The Royal Ballet Company. Physically we couldn't have been better matched, and this was his first foray into Sir Kenneth MacMillan's work. He was perfect for the part.

———

Photo by Anthony Crickmay/Camera Press London

JUNE 1992

The photo below is from a curtain call in Tokyo, taken by a loyal fan.

———

Photo by Mr Usui

THE PRINCE OF PAGODAS

This ballet was basically a total game changer for me in 1989, at the start of my career. I had actually met Sir Kenneth MacMillan, briefly, in 1986 while I was still at The Royal Ballet School and had danced in a performance of his ballet *Concerto* (choreographed to Shostakovich's *Piano Concerto No. 2 in F*). But although I knew who Kenneth was, I had no idea that just a few years later my life would change so much, thanks to this exceptional man.

When I graduated from the school in 1987, I didn't go straight into The Royal Ballet but into its touring Company at the Sadler's Wells Royal Ballet. I wasn't at all disappointed by this, because it was so great to have a job and to be dancing professionally. I got pushed further and faster being in the touring Company and danced roles that I otherwise might not have done, and even got to dance a Principal role in MacMillan's *Elite Syncopations*, which was a sort of test of my ability and agility for his work.

Before the end of the 1988 season, I was asked to go and see Sir Peter Wright, who was my Director at Sadler's Wells Royal Ballet. Working in partnership with Sir Kenneth, who was resident choreographer at The Royal Ballet, they had been in to see a rehearsal of ours, and when Peter and I met he told me that Kenneth wanted to produce a new, three-act ballet, with me in the lead role. This ballet was *The Prince of the Pagodas*, originally choreographed and produced by John Cranko in 1957, with music specially commissioned from Benjamin Britten. Because of his great love of John Cranko's work, it had been a long held ambition of Kenneth's to restore the ballet to the repertoire and he had been working with the novelist and travel writer Colin Thubron to retell the story. Suddenly my life changed and I moved to the resident Company at Covent Garden; immediately we started work on the new version.

The basic story is that of an aging King who divides his kingdom between his two daughters, Princess Epine and Princess Rose. When Epine's suitors prefer Rose, she is banished to the Land of the Pagodas, where she meets the Salamander Prince. Macmillan created the role of Princess Rose for me when I was only 19, so it was a huge compliment that he thought I was up to it. Britten's music is extraordinary and uses the mysterious and sensual gamelan music of Bali. The choreography is basically classical but with an exacting MacMillan twist, so technically it's quite demanding for a dancer, while the story's great drama and beauty also has to be realised.

The year before, Kenneth had unfortunately suffered a serious heart attack and so work on his new ballet was extended to almost a year before it premiered. This was very unusual and a real luxury for us to have this extra time with Kenneth, perfecting the choreography. I just remember working as hard as I could and that all I wanted to do, really, was to impress him. I was very fortunate, too, to be working with Jonathan Cope, who had worked extensively with Kenneth before and was dancing the role of the Salamander Prince. Jonathan was so supportive and helpful to me, constantly explaining that I needed to pace myself, not to over

Sir Kenneth MacMillan
NOVEMBER 1989
The De Valois Studio in Barons Court

This photo was taken during the rehearsals for *The Prince of the Pagodas*. Kenneth looking quite happy, which was unusual given that he rarely showed his emotions. In the old studios of The Royal Ballet Company in Barons Court, London.

Photo by Herbie Knott

Rehearsing *The Prince of the Pagodas*
NOVEMBER 1989
The De Valois Studio in Barons Court

I often showed my nerves through smiling. Getting
to know Sir Kenneth MacMillan and working with
one of my most favourite partners, Jonathan Cope.

Photos by Herbie Knott

exert myself and give 110 per cent to every step or solo or *pas de deux*, or else I wouldn't last the course. But I was so committed to giving it my absolute all and rewarding the confidence Kenneth had placed in me that I couldn't help it. I was also aware that this might be a once in a lifetime opportunity, and if I didn't make a success of it I might never work with him – or anyone else! – again.

The premiere of Kenneth's new production of *The Prince of the Pagodas* was on the 7th of December 1989 in Covent Garden – well, I sensed even then that it would probably set the tone for the rest of my career, and it certainly showed me what was needed to stay at the top of my profession. By getting to know and work with the incomparable Sir Kenneth MacMillan, I was privileged to gain invaluable instruction from one of ballet's great geniuses.

Rehearsing *The Prince of the Pagodas*
NOVEMBER 1989

Photos by Herbie Knott

Rehearsing *The Prince of the Pagodas*
NOVEMBER 1989
The De Valois Studio in Barons Court

A full call of the whole Royal Ballet Company.
Everybody is waiting for their turn to perform,
under the watchful eye of Kenneth MacMillan.

———

Photos by Herbie Knott

On Stage at the Royal Opera House
7TH DECEMBER 1989

The photograph on the left shows myself and my jester, Tetsuya Kumakawa, the renowned Japanese male dancer. He is now like a movie star in Japan.

Photo by Glenn Copus/Rex Shutterstock

The photo above is from the premiere of *The Prince of the Pagodas*. There is a visible sense of relief on our faces at the end of a big show. Just minutes after this picture was taken and with the whole company on stage, our Director, Anthony Dowell, announced that I was promoted to Principal.

David M. Bennett/Getty Images

Illuminations
APRIL 1996

Illuminations was originally created in 1950, choreographed by Sir Frederick Ashton, with scenery and costumes by Cecil Beaton and music by Benjamin Britten. The ballet is based on poems by Arthur Rimbaud called *Les Illuminations* (1871–1872). This is such a wonderfully eccentric ballet and my role as Sacred Love was challenging but it also had the added difficulty of costume changes for every scene.

Photos by Bill Cooper/ArenaPal

Les Rendezvous
29TH FEBRUARY 2000

Les Rendezvous was originally premiered in 1933
and was choreographed by Sir Frederick Ashton.
The scenery and costumes for this revival were
designed by Sir Anthony Dowell. His modern
designs completely transformed the look and feel
of this unique and iconic choreography. I loved
the physical challenge of this ballet. It was first
choreographed on the petite Dame Alicia Markova,
so as a tall dancer it was wonderful to have the
opportunity to perform it.

Left: photo by Henrietta Butler/Alamy
Above: photo by Eric P. Richmond/ArenaPal

La Bayadère
27TH MAY 1989
The Royal Opera House Stage

My first Principal role in a large classic with
The Royal Ballet Company. The role is Gamzatti
and I danced it with the beautiful Russian ballerina
Altynai Asylmuratova and the Bolshoi Ballet star
Irek Mukhamedov. This photo shows me backstage
during a nervous dress rehearsal the day before
the first night.

Photo © Leslie E. Spatt

Swan Lake
3RD FEBRUARY 1990
The Royal Opera House Stage

The photo opposite is from Sir Anthony Dowell's
production of *Swan Lake* and my first performance
as Odette/Odile at the age of 20.

Photo © Leslie E. Spatt

REHEARSING SWAN LAKE *with Sir Anthony Dowell*

The world premiere of Anthony Dowell's production of *Swan Lake* was in 1987, the year after he started as Director of The Royal Ballet. I first danced the Odette/Odile role in 1990 when I was 20, partnered by Jonathan Cope as my Prince Siegfried. It was my first three-act classic as a Principal, and as part of my preparation I had two days of being rehearsed by Dame Margot Fonteyn, which was a real privilege. I thought she was going to drill me on technique and artistry, but instead she emphasised that every step is telling the story, saying 'Don't try and be the Swan, you are always the woman first'. Learning that the narrative is primarily told through the moves themselves, gave me a deeper understanding of how perfectly the choreography and Tchaikovsky's score are intertwined. The whole composition from the solo to the *pas de deux* to the coda (the finale) is so well structured. It is such a classically beautiful ballet, which is why I think you never tire of it and its popularity continues to this day.

The lead role of Odette/Odile was initially created for two ballerinas and premiered at the Bolshoi Theatre in Moscow in 1877. The role demands great stamina and technique as well as dramatic interpretation, playing to different strengths in order to bring the contrasting roles of Odette and Odile to life.

I was very fortunate that as a student in 1987, I appeared in Anthony's brand new production of *Swan Lake* as a lady-in-waiting to the Queen in Act Three, so I got to watch a number of different ballerinas dance the Black Swan/Odile role close up. I learnt so much being able to watch night after night, and to see all these different performances and this experience gave me a real insight to the complexities of what is required by the Principal ballerina in this role.

In these photographs here, I am being rehearsed by Anthony for the production of *Swan Lake* in 1992. I admired him so much both as a dancer and as my Director, it was always a great privilege to work with him or have him in the studio during rehearsals. In this production, I was partnered by Zoltán Solymosi. We were very new to each other at this point, but Zoltán couldn't have been more perfect in terms of height which made things more balanced. Anthony had an extraordinary eye for detail. He would never let you make things fussy or forced. He taught me how to keep my performances real, how to keep the choreography as pure as possible and also how to make the human emotion of the story travel across the vast space of the stage to really connect with the audience.

Here we are rehearsing the *pas de deux* in Act Two. It's very long, almost 10 minutes, and is where Odette is getting to know and trust Prince Siegfried and the sequence just builds so very tenderly and in such a soulful manner.

I danced *Swan Lake* many times over the years, but like many ballerinas I was never absolutely satisfied with what I was producing, because as an artist I always wanted to perfect my dancing and give more. For the ballerina, *Swan Lake* presents one of the most compelling challenges; it has such depth and is so rewarding to dance. Working with Anthony and dancing this role are always inextricably linked for me.

Swan Lake Rehearsal
1992
The Ashton Studio in Barons Court

Rehearsing with my director, Sir Anthony Dowell. Having performed *Swan Lake* for quite a few years, in this season's performances I worked with my new partner, the Hungarian Principal, Zoltán Solymosi.

Photo by Reg Wilson/Rex Shutterstock

Swan Lake Rehearsal
1993
The Ashton Studio in Barons Court

The smallest details are important, they project
great emotion and narrative and Anthony's eye
never missed a thing.
———

Photos by Reg Wilson/Rex Shutterstock

For the ballerina, *Swan Lake* presents one of the most compelling challenges; it has such depth and is so rewarding to dance. Working with Anthony and dancing this role are always inextricably linked for me.

Swan Lake Rehearsal
1993
The Ashton Studio in Barons Court, London

Photo by Reg Wilson/Rex Shutterstock

THE SLEEPING BEAUTY *with Dame Ninette de Valois*

This photo of Dame Ninette de Valois was taken when she visited us backstage after a performance of *The Sleeping Beauty*. Dame Ninette founded The Royal Ballet in 1931. Here she is aged 98, and she was still very much a force to be reckoned with. This was Sir Anthony Dowell's new production of the ballet which had premiered at the John F. Kennedy Center for Performing Arts in Washington, D.C. on 6th April 1994, before opening at the Royal Opera House later that year. Significantly, it was Dame Ninette who had taken The Royal Ballet's original production of *The Sleeping Beauty* to the United States in 1949, with Dame Margot Fonteyn dancing the role of Princess Aurora.

We were aware that Dame Ninette was coming to the performance but it was still extraordinary when she came backstage. I knew she would have some constructive comments to make, despite her poor eyesight sometimes confusing which ballerina was which. You can see from the photo, she was still extremely sharp and 100 per cent committed to ballet. She was someone for whom there were never any excuses – being tired certainly wasn't an option – but she would have known better than anyone how exhausting the role of Princess Aurora is.

The photo always reminds me of the old ballet books. All of us are in our Act Three costumes, which had been newly designed for this production by Maria Bjornson, best known for her designs for *The Phantom of the Opera*. This is a very important photo for me, to be on stage with the founder of The Royal Ballet, and having just danced Princess Aurora in *The Sleeping Beauty*, a ballet that she had used to make the Company internationally famous in 1949.

Dame Ninette de Valois
21ST FEBRUARY 1996

Sir Anthony Dowell's production of *The Sleeping Beauty* premiered at The John F. Kennedy Center for Performing Arts in Washington, D.C. in April 1994. This photo was taken two years later on our home stage at The Royal Opera House. Pictured with my fellow artists, Sarah Wildor, Deborah Bull, myself, Nicola Roberts and Belinda Hatley.

Photo by Nils Jorgensen/Rex Shutterstock

Rehearsing Petipa's *The Sleeping Beauty*
JANUARY 1993

The photo shows me working 'intensely' with my partner, Jonathan Cope, while being guided by my coach Donald MacCleary. When a ballet is so strenuous and physically and mentally demanding, as *The Sleeping Beauty* is, you have to take any opportunity to laugh and release some stress.

*Photo by Ken Towner/*Evening Standard*/ Rex Shutterstock*

2

PROMOTION EN POINTE

ROYAL BALLET POSTERS
Pursuit
Les Biches
La Bayadère
Manon
Romeo & Juliet

WHITE CLIFFS OF BIRLING GAP

THE ROYAL BALLET

A THRILLING PROGRAMME OF MODERN BRITISH BALLET

**David Bintley's
GALANTERIES**
music Wolfgang Amadè Mozart
design Jan Blake

**Ashley Page's
PURSUIT**
music Colin Matthews
design Jack Smith

**Kenneth MacMillan's
GLORIA**
music Francis Poulenc
design Andy Klunder

Royal Opera House
Covent Garden

April 28; May 9, 15 at 7.30pm; May 1, 2 at 8.00pm; April 28 at 2.30pm. **BOX OFFICE: 01-240 1066/1911** tickets available

Pursuit
APRIL 1990

Photographed with Stuart Cassidy
Ballet by Ashley Page

*Photo by Jimmy Wormser/courtesy
of Royal Opera House collections/
designed by Bostock & Pollitt*

ROYAL BALLET POSTERS

It was always a privilege to be featured on a promotional poster and as a student, I have to say it was something of an ambition of mine because I equated being featured on a poster as having made it in some way. It really does give you a sense of pride in your work, especially when your dance Company is The Royal Ballet.

PURSUIT

This Ashley Page ballet was created in 1987 and the role I danced had been created on my good friend, the Principal ballerina Fiona Chadwick. I danced it in 1990 with Stuart Cassidy, a former classmate (pictured opposite). It was a very cool, contemporary piece of work, which the costumes reflect with their striking, bright colours.

This was one of my first posters so it was a real thrill to be selected. Shot by Jimmy Wormser, this inspirational American photographer was a huge ballet fan and did a lot of The Royal Ballet's beautiful photography. As it turned out, this would be the first of many photographs of me taken by Jimmy. He was such a wonderful character and we became firm friends.

The first time I saw the poster on the wall at a tube station going in to work was amazing, turning a corner and seeing it there, smack on the wall. What wasn't quite so great was to see the graffiti that had been added a couple of weeks later. Someone had taken a big black pen and given me a moustache and boobs and Stuart's physique had been similarly enhanced, shall we say. After the initial excitement, this gave me a shock and my pleasure in seeing the poster for the first time took a bit of a knock. But that's life, although it didn't occur to me then that posters would be a continuing feature of my working life.

ROMEO AND JULIET

I had always, always wanted to dance Juliet, but I never thought I would. My Director at the time, Anthony Dowell, thought it was not a role that would suit me because Juliet is thought to be so young, about 14 years old and I was tall. However, the choreographer Kenneth MacMillan was keen for me to dance the role in spite of my height, because he was convinced I had the ability in my acting to portray a young girl in love for the first time. His confidence in me was very important in my believing I could make a success of it.

Jonathan Cope was my Romeo for this production in 1993. He was a wonderful partner and it was particularly reassuring to dance with him; he reduced the apprehension I had with the role and helped me relax during those early performances. This was another shoot with the photographer Sheila Rock (see page 52). We wanted to create the intensely romantic mood between Romeo and Juliet, in our faces as well as our posture, which would reflect what people remember from that beautiful balcony *pas de deux* and MacMillan's wonderful choreography.

In creating any image, you have to reflect that you are a classical dancer first but here the acting role needed to be dominant. Sheila asked me to put my arm up in this sensitive and tender gesture towards Romeo, but it made me rather self-conscious about my armpit (I always had a thing about my armpits!) and how this might look on the poster. So Jonathan suggested he put his hand there. I was afraid this would look contrived but, actually, it works really well because when you look at the embrace, all you see is the narrative between Romeo and Juliet, which embodies their love story.

LA BAYADÈRE

This was one of my long-standing roles. I always enjoyed dancing the temple dancer Nikiya, in this iconic 19th century Russian ballet. This particular production was created by Natalia Makarova in 1980, and when I danced it I actually got to work with this legendary ballerina. It was also a role I danced as Guest Principal at the Mariinsky Ballet in St Petersburg in 1998, and with the Australian Ballet.

This poster, photographed by Bill Cooper (see page 54), was for the 2003 production and it was just after I returned from maternity leave, following the birth of my first daughter Phoebe. I was really quite nervous because it is a role that demands real confidence and great strength and flexibility in your technique, and when we did our first full call with the whole Company even Natalia Makarova was in attendance. I was very conscious of all this.

When I danced my first solo and a bit of the *pas de deux*, to my great surprise everyone applauded which was quite lovely. Even Makarova looked happy. It was a real confidence booster, supporting my return to dancing a major role again after having had a baby and time away. As a Principal, it's never easy to come back after a break and step straight back into a demanding role, so I will never forget the reassuring warmth of that applause. This poster always reminds me of how important it is to have the support from the Company and your colleagues. It's very special to me.

MANON

I had originally been partnered with the Russian dancer Irek Mukhamedov to dance the role of *Manon* in 1991. Its choreographer Kenneth MacMillan thought it would work well for us because it had been created for Dame Antoinette Sibley and Anthony Dowell, and he thought that it would suit our partnership too. It didn't work out, which was a shame, in spite of us dancing successfully together in *Winter Dreams*, roles created for us by MacMillan just the year before. I was pretty devastated by this cast change, so early in my career as a Principal, and I wondered if I would ever get to dance this fantastic role. In 1993 I did get the chance to dance my first Manon, this time with Zoltán Solymosi in the role of Des Grieux. A very fiery, charismatic, Hungarian dancer, we were physically well suited because Zoltán is tall. It was wonderful to be dancing the role and to feature in the poster (see page 55).

I don't think Zoltán had done many photo shoots before and he seemed quite uncomfortable with it, which made me feel quite nervous too. Sheila Rock, the photographer, was keen for us to depict the intensity of feeling between our characters. She kept trying to inject a little more passion into things, suggesting that he kiss me, kiss my neck or appear to kiss me in some way, but I could tell this was making Zoltán really embarrassed. I felt awkward about it as well. Some of the photos taken actually look much too coy for the reality of the story. This all made the shoot quite a tough one, but in the end I think Sheila got a picture that is true to the relationship between Manon and her lover.

THE ROYAL BALLET

A VIBRANT PROGRAMME OF MODERN BALLET

AGON

STOICS QUARTET

NEW BALLET

SYMPHONY IN C

Agon
APRIL 1991

Photographed with
Christopher Saunders
Ballet by George Balanchine

*Photo by David Buckland/V&A
Archive/courtesy of Royal Opera
House Collections*

20, 21, 26 NOVEMBER 3, 6, 7 DECEMBER AT 7.30PM

BOX OFFICE 071 - 240 1066/1911

ROYAL
OPERA
HOUSE
Covent Garden

THE ROYAL BALLET

ROMEO AND JULIET

Jonathan Cope as Romeo, Darcey Bussell as Juliet. Photograph: Sheila Rock

RE-STAGING SPONSORED (1975)
BY GUINNESS PEAT GROUP

17 22 FEBRUARY
10 20 APRIL AT 7.30PM
15 APRIL AT 2PM AND 7PM

The
ROYAL
BALLET

ROYAL OPERA HOUSE · TELEPHONE 0171-304 4000

Funded by
THE
ARTS
COUNCIL
OF ENGLAND

Romeo & Juliet
FEBRUARY/APRIL 1993

Photographed with Jonathan Cope
Ballet by Sir Kenneth MacMillan

Photo © Sheila Rock/courtesy
of Royal Opera House Collections

LES BICHES

Les Biches is a wonderful one-act ballet that dates back to 1924. Choreographed by the innovative Bronislava Nijinska (who originally danced my role), for the Ballets Russes de Sergei Diaghilev. Its world premiere was in January 1924 at the Théâtre de Monte-Carlo, and its Royal Ballet premiere at The Royal Opera House was in December 1964. It's the story of a house party in the South of France in the 1920s, and *Les Biches* translates to 'doe' (female deer), which was a slang term for coquettish women. David Scheinmann shot the photograph for this poster (see pages 56–59), when I danced the role of the party hostess for the first time in 1991.

It's a surprisingly elaborate costume to dance in, with all the strings of pearls, the feathered headdress and an amazing cigarette holder, all rather louche and decadent in style. It's also an incredibly demanding piece of choreography, difficult and exhausting to the point where I would sometimes wonder how I would get through it. It never got any easier however hard I rehearsed and I've danced it several times. You even had a to smoke a real cigarette on stage; it was very important not to inhale the smoke in case you had a sudden coughing fit, because the demands of the choreography meant that you were out of breath through most of the ballet!

My hair was very long then and when I was having it styled for the shot it took just under an hour to create the 1920s Marcel wave that was fashionable at the time, in an effort to keep the look very authentic. There was the makeup girl, photographer and everyone else, waiting and waiting for the hairdresser and it just took ages. I only had to sit for the shot, not dance, unlike most other occasions, but it took a while to get a shot that everyone was happy with. One of the problems, as David reminded me, was that I tend to smile a lot, so keeping a straight face with a very direct look at the camera was difficult, but I needed to depict the character I was playing. So while the character didn't feel much like me, I think we achieved something quite special in this poster.

'Dark deeds in the Himalayas...
a tragedy of love, murder and revenge'

LA BAYADÈRE

17 OCTOBER – 13 NOVEMBER 2003

THE ROYAL BALLET
COVENT GARDEN

Natalia Makarova after Marius Petipa | Revival sponsored (2002) by The Friends of Covent Garden

Cast: TAMARA ROJO, CARLOS ACOSTA, MARIANELA NUÑEZ |17 22 Oct 13 Nov|, ROBERTA MARQUEZ, IVAN PUTROV, DEIRDRE CHAPMAN |18 Oct 12 Nov|
DARCEY BUSSELL, ROBERTO BOLLE, ZENAIDA YANOWSKY |21 31 Oct|, ALINA COJOCARU, JOHAN KOBBORG, LAURA MORERA |1 5 Nov|
MARIANELA NUÑEZ, THIAGO SOARES, LAUREN CUTHBERTSON |3 Nov|, JAIMIE TAPPER, IÑAKI URLEZAGA, ZENAIDA YANOWSKY |10 Nov|

BOOKING OPENS 18 AUGUST | Darcey Bussell as Nikiya (Photograph : Bill Cooper) | Designed by Dewynters

La Bayadère
2003

Ballet by Natasha Makarova

*Photo by Bill Cooper/ArenaPal/
designed by Dewynters*

THE ROYAL BALLET

Manon

Darcey Bussell and Zoltán Solymosi in *Manon* Photograph: Sheila Rock

Manon

FEBRUARY 1993

Photographed with Zoltán Solymosi
Ballet by Sir Kenneth MacMillan

*Photo © Sheila Rock/courtesy
of Royal Opera House Collections*

THE ROYAL BALLET

Les Biches

JUNE 1991

Ballet by Bronislava Nijinska

Left: photo by David Scheinmann
Right: photo by David Scheinmann/
courtesy of Royal Opera House
Collections

LES BICHES   SCÈNES DE BALLET   LES NOCES

5, 7, 10, 11, 12, 13, 14 June at 8pm   Box Office: 071-240 1066/1911

ROYAL OPERA HOUSE Covent Garden

Les Biches
5TH JUNE 1991
Ballet by Bronislava Nijinska

In these photos, I'm on the Royal Opera House
stage dancing the role of 'The Hostess' in the
ballet *Les Biches*. The ballet was first created in
1924 and created on Nijinska herself. The music
for this work was composed by Francis Poulenc.

———————

Above: photo by David Scheinmann
Right: photo by Laurie Lewis

Car Park in Hammersmith
30TH JUNE 1997
Frank Dale & Stepsons, London

The Royal Opera House was closed between
1997 and 1999 while it was being renovated and
expanded, so The Royal Ballet was on the road.
Fellow Principal Stuart Cassidy (pictured) and I
were to open the season with *The Sleeping Beauty*,
hence the advertising campaign to 'follow us' to
the Hammersmith Apollo. My old friend Cassidy,
is still dancing to this day, mainly in Japan.

Photo by Laurie Lewis

The Nutcracker
2001

Ballet by Sir Peter Wright

Photo by Eric Richmond/courtesy of Royal Opera House Collections/ designed by Dewynters

Sylvia
2004

Photographed with Jonathan Cope
Ballet by Sir Frederick Ashton

Photo by Andy Whale/courtesy of
Royal Opera House Collections/
designed by Dewynters

WHITE CLIFFS OF BIRLING GAP

Between 2005 and 2012 the Royal Opera House ran a promotional campaign of posters shot by photographer Jason Bell, featuring both ballet and opera stars in their countries of origin. These were a series of really dramatic shots, for example, dancer Carlos Acosta was photographed on the beach in Cuba and the soprano Liping Zhang in the snow in the front of the Jianyang Fort, China. Being English, I was photographed in front of the Birling Gap in East Sussex, maybe not quite so exotic but very poignant and striking.

My poster was one of the first to be photographed and I remember being quite surprised that we were going to do the shoot outside of London. Being a Londoner born and bred, I had half-expected to be photographed near Big Ben or in Trafalgar Square. However, I am so glad that East Sussex was chosen. The cliffs are so imposing and beautiful and they made a fantastically dramatic backdrop.

Of course, being in a remote location was always going to provide some obstacles! Fortunately it was one of those perfect early summer days, with very good light, which you can't always guarantee in an English summer. We had the use of a small caravan quite close to the beach, where I got into costume, and did my hair and makeup. The tutu was an old one with a very nice velvet bodice, but it was quite thick and boned and structured, so was rather hot in the sunshine.

With my hair slicked firmly into place to stop any breeze messing it up, I walked to the beach in flip flops. I then had to get my pointe shoes on. Fortunately one of the crew had brought a piece of plywood for me to sit on, so I didn't get my costume wet or covered in sand or seaweed. Every time we moved to a different location on the beach, The Royal Ballet's Head of Press, Janine Limberg, had to piggyback me there to save time so I didn't have to keep taking my pointe shoes on and off. Poor thing!

We opted for a simple pose because the beach was too rocky with lots of little pools, which made it too precarious to attempt a dramatic jump or anything overly adventurous. Standing *en pointe* I sunk into the sand and my feet started to look rather short! My pointe shoes, being made only of satin and canvas, began to get very soft from the wet sand and heat of the day. They could have easily fallen apart and foolishly I had only bought one new pair. Again the piece of plywood came to the rescue and I stood on that instead. I didn't remember any sunscreen so my nose began to get pinker and pinker and of course we also had to watch the time because of the tide.

I think the contrast of this simple, classic pose worked well with my dark tutu set against the backdrop of the beach and the white cliffs. At the end of the main shoot I cooled my feet in a rock pool, which achieved another shot. The Royal Opera House used it for promotion but not for the main poster (see page 67).

Seven Sisters Cliffs
2005
Birling Gap, East Sussex

Photo by *Jason Bell/Camera Press London*

Seven Sisters Cliffs
2005
Birling Gap, East Sussex

Former Head of Press for The Royal Ballet,
Janine Limberg, is shown giving me a piggyback
ride in the contact sheet, opposite.

———

Photos by Jason Bell/Camera Press London

3

MOMENTS FROM THE LENS

ANTHONY CRICKMAY

I already knew of Anthony Crickmay and his work with The Royal Ballet because as a student I had his beautiful posters on my wall, so to be photographed by him was hugely exciting. I was very fortunate to work with Anthony many times over the years, first when I was 19 on a fashion shoot for *The Sunday Times*. Anthony is a real fan of the ballet. He has an innate understanding of a dancer's body and lines, so he always knows exactly when we won't be happy with a photo! One of the great things about his studio, where this photo with Carlos Acosta was shot, is that it has a sprung floor installed especially for photographing dancers, which protects our bodies when we jump.

The idea behind this photograph with Carlos, the award-winning Principal Guest Artist at The Royal Ballet between 2003–2016, was to give a sense of the diverse work and repertoire of the company, using us to represent the contrasting roles that exist in classical and contemporary dance. I represented the typical ideal of an English ballerina, alongside this dynamic, exciting Cuban dancer, with whom I'd been partnered for numerous ballets. We were really happy to be working together with Anthony on this.

My tutu was from a Balanchine ballet, *Symphony in C*, and had originally been white but it was dyed red for this photo. My initial thought was how shocking – this beautiful tutu, dyed red! That was the point, though, to show a heightened visual contrast between us in the photo; my skin looking so white against the vibrant red of my tutu and Carlos looking so dark, dramatic and contemporary. This contrast was extended further by my classical pose and Carlos's powerful and graceful jump, for which he was so famous. As an image of the versatility of The Royal Ballet, it is perfect.

Looking at this photo you may think that we were photographed separately and the images edited together, but this picture was taken exactly as it appears. This was much trickier than it looks, and was all about timing. I was positioned in the foreground and had to achieve my balance when Carlos hit the highest point of his jump, which I couldn't actually see because he was behind me. To achieve the shot Anthony wanted, I was very conscious that I would need to get the visual shape of my pose right, that the line of my legs would mirror the line of my arms, and these would also mirror those of Carlos behind me, with my pose complementing his. It was also important that our bodies didn't cross and look messy but beautifully fluid and to be caught mid-sequence. Not easy!

We had to do it over and over again to get the shot precisely right. I remember I was desperate to change sides, to work my other leg. Carlos must have felt the same. When you dance, you're constantly moving. It's not usual to repeat the same movement and hold it momentarily. After a while I remember I could feel my hamstring was ready to seize up into a cramp. The photo captured the extraordinary elevation of Carlos's jump. In a photographic studio there's seldom enough room to do justice to a jump like that, but the sprung floor and Anthony's talent (often lying on the floor to get the best angle) made all the difference.

Royal Ballet Company Advertising
2ND DECEMBER 1999

Carlos Acosta and myself posed for Anthony Crickmay in his famous studio in Fulham Broadway, London. The photo turned into a piece of advertising for the season's repertoire.

Photo by Anthony Crickmay/Camera Press London

Chiffon Ease
2ND APRIL 1998

A shoot for *The Sunday Times* with Anthony
Crickmay. I totally trusted his judgement on all
of the images we were trying to produce. All of the
outfits were made of chiffon and easy to move in.

Photos by Anthony Crickmay/Camera Press London

Anthony is a real fan of the ballet. He has an innate understanding of a dancer's body and lines, so he always knows exactly when we won't be happy with a photo!

Herman Schmerman
10TH MAY 1998

From the front page of the culture section of *The Sunday Times* alongside a story about the upcoming season of The Royal Ballet Company. My partner Adam Cooper and I are wearing costumes designed by Gianni Versace for a ballet called *Herman Schmerman*, created by William Forsythe. In order to keep my skirt in place we used the handy trick of double-sided tape attached to my leg. Perhaps Adam should have used it too.

Photo by Anthony Crickmay/Camera Press London

GAP Advertisement
1990

This was an advertising shoot for GAP during the time that I was performing in *The Prince of the Pagodas* with my friend Tetsuya 'Teddy' Kumakawa – the horribly talented Japanese ballet dancer. We were asked to wear GAP clothes, naturally, but Teddy insisted on wearing his own designer jeans (which obviously didn't go down very well with the GAP folks). This was my first time working with Annie Leibovitz and I felt incredibly apprehensive, even with Teddy there. She couldn't have been more charming and we had a lot of fun creating a very relaxed series of photos, rather than balletic poses in jeans.

Photos © Annie Leibovitz/courtesy of the artist

GAP Advertisement
1990

This is not what we were out to achieve, but as Teddy was being such a flirt, I had to give him a gentle punch to put him in his place.

Photo © Annie Leibovitz/courtesy of the artist

ARTHUR ELGORT, VOGUE

As a dancer you don't get to do that many big magazine photo shoots, but probably the biggest one I ever did was when I was just 20 years old, for British *Vogue* in 1989, with the extraordinary photographer Arthur Elgort. Although his reputation was for beautiful and innovative fashion photography, he also had a great interest in ballet. I was very excited to be invited to work with him on this shoot in New York.

Arthur was also photographing another ballerina alongside me, Cynthia Harvey, who I knew. She was with The American Ballet Theatre (where she had danced with Mikhail Baryshnikov in the filmed version of *Don Quixote* in 1983) and had been a Principal Guest Artist at The Royal Ballet when I first joined the Company, so it was lovely to be working with her again.

The Royal Ballet had just completed a North American tour and I stayed on in New York for the four-day shoot – four days, almost unheard of today – in the largest photographic studio I've ever worked in. I would meet Cynthia every morning to take a 90-minute ballet class with David Howard (one of the most famous dance teachers in New York), which set us up for a day of creating dance images in Arthur's studio. It was incredibly demanding to combine a fashion shoot with ballet and not ruin our bodies in the process!

We had the most stunning clothes, some heavily brocaded, some very diaphanous, wonderful fabrics and textures, and all were just beautiful. It was a fantastically elaborate process, too: the clothes, the hair and makeup, the styling, and the time taken to work out, design and light the poses for the shots.

Arthur's three-year old daughter, Sophie, also joined us for some of the pictures. She looked divine, so pretty with her white blonde hair and tutus, imitating every move we made when we were jumping or posing. She was so full of energy, she never seemed to tire!

I loved the way Arthur worked, with his love of ballet and attention to detail; it was like creating a whole ballet production. I was very spoilt by such an exceptional experience and will never forget those few days in New York.

Vogue
DECEMBER 1989

Photographed in New York for *Vogue*, I am with Sophie, daughter of the famed photographer Arthur Elgort. She was watching from the sidelines and couldn't help but join in. Absolutely adorable in my gold pointe shoes.

Photo by Arthur Elgort

Vogue
DECEMBER 1989

To achieve such physical ballet moves I did a ballet class in NYC each morning before we started the shoot. On the left-hand photo you can see the large curved canvas behind me. I had to be very careful to not put my foot through it as I repeated the grand sissonne jump over and over so that Arthur could capture it at full height.

—————

Photos by Arthur Elgort

I loved the way Arthur worked, his love of ballet and attention to detail; it was like creating a whole ballet production. I was very spoilt by such an exceptional experience and will never forget those few days in New York.

Vogue
DECEMBER 1989

With my friend Cynthia Harvey and Arthur Elgort's daughter, Sophie. Cynthia was a Principal ballerina at American Ballet Theatre and is now Artistic Director of The Jacqueline Kennedy Onassis School at ABT. We are both in the *penché* ballet position.

Photo by Arthur Elgort

Flying Leap?
2002

Working with Chris Nash on this shoot was a lot
of fun because I was in a very tight, beaded, red
dress that I physically could not move in. We liked
the dress so much that Chris sat me in a chair and
we created moves, then he retouched the chair out
of the photograph. It took a lot of pressure off
me and I didn't have to exhaust myself.

Photo by Chris Nash

Hats
1990

I love the way a hat can immediately create
character and fun. In this shoot I wore a collection
of striking hats by the extremely talented milliner
Philip Treacy, whose creativity I instantly fell in
love with. I was very fortunate to wear his hats
when I collected my OBE at Buckingham Palace
and a stunning feathered hat when leaving for
my honeymoon.

Photo by Clive Arrowsmith/Camera Press London

JOHN SWANNELL, GOLD CAMPAIGN

A series of twenty-four photographs were taken of me by acclaimed photographer John Swannell for a World Gold Council advertising campaign in 2000. They show me wearing pieces of contemporary jewellery that had featured in, and won, the Council's first ever Gold Virtuosi International Jewellery Awards earlier that year. The campaign appeared in magazines including *Vanity Fair* and *Vogue*, and the Virtuosi Awards have since become known as the Oscars of gold jewellery design, showcasing new work by contemporary goldsmiths from around the world.

All the jewellery selected for the photos were very much statement pieces. They were works of art and extraordinarily beautiful, but some were difficult to wear. I remember that many of the earrings were heavy and quite painful after a while.

Hilary Alexander, who was then Fashion Director at the *Telegraph* newspaper, was the stylist for the shoot and wanted to have a series of very different, contrasting styles to reflect the brief that gold jewellery is for *all* women. She had very specific ideas for each piece, and this made each shot uniquely produced and staged. Some shots were moody, some very young and cheeky, some balletic, some elegant, but each one was meticulously conceived and created by John and Hilary. Jonathan Malone did my hair and makeup and everything was planned down to the smallest detail.

We went to four sites over a number of days to take the photos – I can't remember now how I fitted it all in as I was dancing fulltime too! These included a Lake District location in a very beautiful house, along with studio shoots in London. The piece I'm wearing in the photo with the stripy leg warmers (see page 90) is a piece called *Thando*, hand crafted in 18 carat gold by Renate Kriegler, a final-year BA Fine Arts student at Stellenbosch University, South Africa, which won the top award that year.

Whilst I was just there to model the jewellery, I also needed to convey its character and to promote the possibilities of how it could look or be worn. This made it a really theatrical project and I loved the imaginative aspect of the shoot. I really admired the way John and Hilary complimented each other. Given the freedom by the client to use their collective skill without reservation, they fittingly showcased each extraordinary piece.

Ballerina in Doc Martens
2000

This shoot was styled by Hilary Alexander, and I loved her choice and variety of the outfits.

Photo by John Swannell/Camera Press London

The Punk Dancer

2000

I enjoyed the challenge of posing with such unusual jewellery. In the photo above, wearing ankle bracelets and a tail meant that if I moved at all the piece may well have been damaged. It kept the shoot both interesting and entertaining.

Photos by John Swannell/Camera Press London

Sepia Tones
2000

We had to get creative with our poses to showcase this stunning jewellery. Note the brooch on my bum and the only way of keeping the earrings on was by leaning over in the photo below.

Photos by John Swannell/Camera Press London

Boodles & Dunthorne

29TH JULY 1997

Another nice opportunity to work with John Swannell. A jewellery campaign at the time of the opening of Boodles & Dunthorne's first London store. They sweetly proposed that I arrive at the opening in a Cinderella carriage, wearing my tutu. I declined, thinking I would hold up a lot of traffic in busy Knightsbridge. John kindly gave me this print as a gift.

Photo by John Swannell/courtesy of the Darcey Bussell Collection

Channelling Audrey Hepburn
JANUARY 1997

On the roof of The Dorchester hotel in London.
The shoot was done as an homage to Audrey
Hepburn, who has always been a heroine of mine,
so to create these images was a bit of a dream.
I had to hold on tight to the balloons and my hat
because I was worried that everything might end
up in Hyde Park.

———

Photo by John Stoddart/Getty Images

Mulberry Perfume
1997

I had previously done a campaign with Mulberry
for their homeware and Roger Saul, the effervescent
founder of the company, had asked if I would do
their first perfume advertisement, which I was
thrilled to do. The shoot was at their headquarters
in Somerset.

———

Photo by Tim Richmond/courtesy of Roger Saul/
Mulberry/courtesy of the Darcey Bussell Collection

Mulberry Fashion
1997

It was so lovely to be so natural and not contrived
at all in this shoot. I still wear this dress today
and again I'm photographed at the Mulberry
headquarters in Somerset.

*Photo by Tim Richmond/courtesy of the Darcey
Bussell Collection*

MARIO TESTINO

I worked with Mario Testino for a poster campaign to promote the re-opening of the Royal Opera House, Covent Garden in May 2000. He was, of course, very well known as a fashion photographer and had taken those iconic *Vanity Fair* photos of Diana Princess of Wales in 1997, so I was very thrilled to work with him.

Mario works fast and with a small hand-held camera. He doesn't set anything up but instead works in a very quick, spontaneous way so the shoot feels quite informal and natural.

For someone from whom you might expect a bit of self-importance, considering the success of his career, Mario certainly isn't like that. He is absolutely charming to work with and there's no pressure or stress in the working environment. I'll never forget his cheekiness, how he would put you at ease and that every shoot was fun.

The headshot (opposite) was taken for *Vanity Fair* magazine to celebrate Her Majesty The Queen's Golden Jubilee in 2002, for which there was a gala performance at the Royal Opera House. For this, Jonathan Cope and I danced both the *pas de deux* from Christopher Wheeldon's ballet *Tryst* and Sir Frederick Ashton's *Birthday Offering*. Mario wanted me to look as if I was mid-performance for this photo, so I have the very dramatic stage makeup with pronounced eyeliner, darkened brows and false eyelashes and this eccentric headdress with its stars cascading down the back. My hair is very tightly swept back, on which the headdress is safely secured to make sure that it doesn't move or fall off when I'm dancing, pirouetting and jumping.

I remember thinking that, close up, this photo would look just too theatrical and rather odd, but Mario wanted me to look very authentic, not overly staged and to be true to the idea that I was in full costume just about to perform. It's an example of his personal interpretation and photographic skill.

On a separate shoot, Mario had asked that I wear a very dramatic costume, which is why I appear as Odile, the Black Swan from *Swan Lake* (see page 103). He had again asked that I wear full stage makeup, which is designed to project our features under strong lights to the back of the auditorium, which he loved and he complimented me on that. Other shots he took in this sequence were more formal. The most famous one is probably the shot of me alone, *en pointe* and backstage in front of the lighting rig, that appeared on the walls of London's tube stations and which the National Portrait Gallery purchased for their collection.

The idea for this photo, however, was that I'm backstage waiting to perform, which is why he gave me cup of water, as if I am just there pausing between scenes, chatting and waiting to make my entrance. I'm pictured next to another dancer, Maurice Vodegel-Matzen, and we're in a very relaxed pose, which is actually nothing like it really is backstage during a performance where we are normally struggling to catch our breath and recover our composure for the next scene. But I particularly like the relationship between me and the camera in this one, as if Mario has just asked me a question.

Mario Comes to the Ballet
2002

Mario caught me backstage as I was performing *Birthday Offering*, a ballet by Sir Frederick Ashton. The unusual costume jewellery looks best from the auditorium.

Photo © Mario Testino, Darcey Bussell, London, 2002

For someone from whom you might expect a bit of self-importance, considering the success of his career, Mario certainly isn't like that. He is absolutely charming to work with and there's no pressure or stress in the working environment.

Backstage Refreshment
2002

Recreating a backstage image in my Odile costume from the third act of *Swan Lake* with fellow dancer Maurice Vodegel-Matzen.

———

Photo © Mario Testino, Darcey Bussell,
London, 2002

ESQUIRE PHOTO SHOOT

Quite often a photographer wants to project a different image from the one you're known for, to show a contrasting side to your presumed character. As an artist I was happy not to be typecast and always enjoyed working on something that made a statement of difference.

The photographer on this shoot was John Stoddart, famous for his glamorous photos of actors and models. I'm not exactly sure who decided that I should wear a black leather catsuit, but it was made especially for me. When I first tried it on I thought, 'Wow, this is rather daring and not something I would ever have bought for myself.' My hair at the time was short, so that was also a departure from my usual image.

John kept encouraging me to lower the zip of my catsuit, lower and lower, but that's not really me. I was happy to play a seductive character – and it was certainly entertaining to try! But there's a fine line to keeping it stylish without pushing it too far and that was important to me. Fortunately, John agreed with me – in the end!

Esquire Magazine
1998

———

Photo by John Stoddart/Getty Images

The shoot was for *Esquire* magazine in 1998 and took place at Brands Hatch. I'm such a fan of beautifully designed cars; the car in the shot is a stunning Lamborghini. I have always loved driving so it was incredibly exciting to take such a wonderful car at speed around this famous racetrack. This occurred in spite of the concern of its owner, who insisted on sitting in the passenger seat. It was definitely the thrill of the day for me, perhaps not for him!

The other photo (below) was taken later, although I'm wearing the same catsuit, which was reprised for an Audi shoot in their car showroom. The contrast between the black leather and the white car makes a really striking photo. I also did another promotional shoot for the launch of the Audi A8 4.2 Quattro in 2000, wearing a black leather miniskirt and boots, photographed by Jon Furniss. So the connection between fast cars and me continued!

Audi
2000

In an Audi car showroom in London. I have been very privileged to be a long-term ambassador for Audi.

Photo courtesy of Audi UK

IMPERIAL WAR MUSEUM EXHIBITION OF FORTIES FASHION

In 1997 the Imperial War Museum celebrated the 50th anniversary of Dior's New Look with an exhibition that showcased the fashion of the 1940s. I was delighted to be photographed by Lord Snowdon for the exhibition poster and cover of Colin McDowell's book *Forties Fashion and the New Look*, for which I wrote the foreword and Sir Hardy Amies the introduction. This was something I was really interested in, due to my mother's influence. Her knowledge of this era is vast and she also ran her own fashion boutique in the Kings Road in the late 1960s.

After a morning of rehearsals I zoomed to Tony Snowdon's Battersea studio knowing that he'd be anxious if I was at all late. We had met when I was sixteen for my first ever publicity shot, but that was pure ballet. I was fortunate to be photographed by him many times subsequently, even in his own garden, and the opportunity of working with him was always a thrill.

Towards the end of the war, New York, strongly influenced by Hollywood, had become the temporary fashion capital of the world. For years after the war there was clothes rationing in Europe, make do and mend, homemade cosmetics and women's magazines lending circles, in an effort to keep morale and high fashion alive. Then Paris hit back. Part of this Parisian movement was the Corolle Line, nicknamed the 'New Look', which launched the career of Christian Dior. Some of the initial criticism came from Dior's use of lots of fabric in his designs, which often had very full skirts, while there was still clothes rationing.

For the shoot, I was excited to be wearing one of the original New Look suits, the 'Bar', made by Dior in 1947. The jacket was in palest pink and the skirt in black wool crepe. The only thing missing from the original outfit were the shoes, but I wore a similar pair of vintage 1940s heels. I must admit, however, this famous outfit with its nipped in waist wasn't very comfortable. I was to balance on one of the pillars with the light coming in from the side, replicating an historical look but for the 20th century and posing in the classic way of the models of the 1940s. But it wasn't the easiest of shoots as the atmosphere in the studio was quite tense. Tony always has a very specific idea of what he wanted to achieve in a photo, and sometimes he lost a little patience with his younger assistants, so everyone was running around like crazy to get it right for him.

A few months later I went to the opening of the exhibition at the Imperial War Museum London where the event had models parading in the original 40s clothing. They included a Hollywood costume once worn by Ida Lupino (the pioneering actress and movie director / producer), an evening dress poignantly made of vivid yellow parachute silk and a WAAF Section Officer's uniform cheekily lined in non-regulation scarlet. It was truly exceptional and I loved every minute of it.

The New Look
1997

Photo by Lord Anthony Snowdon/
© The Imperial War Museum
(Art.IWM PST 20400)

Forties Fashion
and the New Look

Photograph by Snowdon

Imperial War Museum

12 FEBRUARY - 31 AUGUST 1997 • OPEN DAILY 10.00am-6.00pm

Lambeth Road London SE1 6HZ • 0171 416 5000

Sponsored by Parfums Christian Dior

Model Darcey Russell
The book *Forties Fashion and the New Look* by Colin McDowell is published by Bloomsbury, price £20.00

JUST THE
THING
FOR FREQUENT
FLYERS.

When you're swanning around the

world you can earn valuable

rewards, including free travel, with

the Membership Rewards™ programme.

And because the Card also offers

travel delay compensation, and

guaranteed hotel reservations, it's

the perfect partner to travel with.

do more.

American Express Advertisement
1999

———

Photo courtesy of Richard Avedon, © The Richard Avedon Foundation/with permission from American Express/Advertising Archives

AMERICAN EXPRESS ADVERTISEMENT

This was part of a 'Best of British' advertising campaign and included various other Brits, like the world heavyweight boxing champion Lennox Lewis. It was shot by the famous fashion and advertising photographer Richard Avedon, who was in his 70s then. Richard's black and white portraits are some of the most recognisable photos taken in the second half of the 20th century, so it was exciting to have the opportunity to work with him.

The idea of the shoot was to make me look like a Londoner, rushing through town with my raincoat and umbrella on my way to catch a plane, hence the passport and air ticket in my other hand. Photographing a balletic leap – a *jeté* – that flies through the air linked the idea that this card would be great for travellers or 'frequent flyers'.

It was very important to me, to get my alignment correct for a classical ballet *jeté*. In order to get the perfect shot, it has to be repeated, which makes it very hard on the legs and body and you have to make sure that you can still walk – or in my case, still dance – the next day. So to help create the photo, but also to preserve my energy, we used a trampoline but that, too, had its own considerations.

Normally, when you dance a *jeté* it occurs as part of a sequence of steps which not only gives you a run up to it but also a natural forward motion. The dynamics of doing this on a trampoline, and doing it in isolation, are very different. I had to adjust to the bounce and elevation that the trampoline gave, to make sure that I hadn't travelled too far forward while trying to achieve the pose. Even the photographer needed to be at the right height to get the right view. It was very technical and that's why repetition was so necessary.

What's more, if the raincoat lifted in the wrong position as I jumped, I looked like I had rounded shoulders, so it had to be stuck to me to stop this happening. To make sure it looked as if the coat was flying out behind me, I had a fan blowing hard at me. I also had to make sure that the umbrella didn't get in the way of my face or stab me when I landed and that I didn't drop the passport and air ticket. And then I had to remember to smile and look natural!

For all these reasons, it was a very tricky photograph to get right and, in the end, we spliced together two photos, as there was no digital adjustment or Photoshop possible then. One, where my legs were perfectly positioned, with the right elevation that I was happy with, and the other photo of my upper body in a good posture with the raincoat and props in the right place that the photographer was happy with. I learnt a lot from this photo shoot: how to make it work for the client but also how to keep it true to the correct position of a balletic pose. I remember that I was given a black American Express card for one year as part of my fee, which made me feel very grown up at the time. It was a shame that my income as a ballerina meant I never really had enough money to use it but I was more than rewarded by the opportunity to do this shoot with the iconic Richard Avedon.

THE LONDON EYE

In January 1999, Joanna Lumley and I broke the ground on the site for the London Eye. Prime Minister Tony Blair later opened it on New Year's Eve 1999. Initially, it was assumed that this controversial Ferris wheel would be a temporary installation for the millennial celebrations, but it proved so popular that it stayed up. British Airways were the sponsors at the time and to promote it I was asked to do a balletic photo in one of the pods, so as we were performing *Swan Lake* at the time and we were to be up in the sky it seemed the right classical image.

The shoot proved to be quite difficult to organise because the wheel operates throughout the day every day, so we had to get this done very early one morning. This meant I had to arrive, in full costume, at about 8.30 in the morning, before the first tourists arrived. As it only takes 30 minutes for the wheel to do a full revolution (without stopping), this makes the opportunity for getting a perfect backdrop quite tight. A lot to pull together for one shot!

First I had to go to the Royal Opera House to get into full makeup, my Odette/White Swan tutu, hair and headdress, tights, pointe shoes, the lot! I then put boots – like those après-ski snow boots – over my shoes, a coat over my costume and jumped into a cab to go from Covent Garden down to London's South Bank. I remember walking to the wheel, past the London Aquarium in the old City Hall building, thinking that I must look like a giant black waddling pear because my tutu was making my coat stick out. There I was, trying – and failing – not to appear too conspicuous.

The next challenge was to work out the shot. I had to consider how high I could get my leg in a classic arabesque in the confined space of the pod, while the team worked out the point where the view of London beyond looked best and then with the camera focused and everything set up, I had to balance long enough to get the shot. Everything felt very odd. I had glass all around me as if there were no boundaries, unlike in a studio. I felt as if I was floating within the clouds with that strange slow momentum of the pod moving. I then had to try and hit that arabesque at exactly the right moment – not easy!

Along with the photographer David White, I was with Janine Limberg. Fortunately Janine was able to hold my hand to support my balance as I moved from fifth position to one leg, because usually a position is only held momentarily in the course of a sequence of movement and you need to capture the sense of that in a photograph. Resting my hand in Janine's meant I could be perfectly centred for the photograph allowing me to keep my leg up to the right height behind me and then, as Janine let go and stepped out of shot at the last second, I could extend my arms into the full pose.

After all of this, we weren't guaranteed good weather of course. Fortunately it was a beautiful day, the light was good, the view of the London backdrop was clear and the white clouds passing across the blue sky were perfect. All of the hard work and fuss paid off.

The London Eye
24TH FEBRUARY 2000

Photo courtesy of David White/
Newscastimages

Portrait with Feathers
APRIL 1993

Designed by Emanuel Ungaro, the weight of this dress was extrordinary because it was beaded from head to toe. I loved this dress but unfortunately I couldn't have ever danced in it, due to its weight and the feathers around the neck. Going into this shoot I was unaware that it was going to be a large spread of about eight photos in *Harper's Bazaar*. Patrick was the most grounded, humble and quiet man, despite his iconic career as a photographer, and how we squeezed this shoot into one day I'll never know.

Photo by Patrick Demarchelier/Hearst Communications Inc.

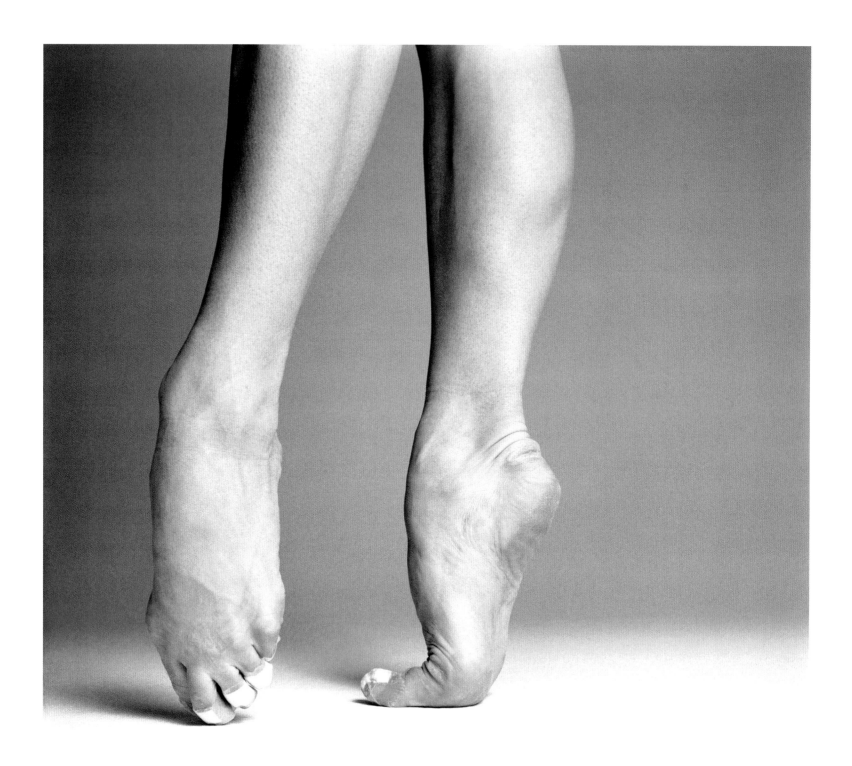

Dancer's Feet

APRIL 1993

Photographer Patrick Demarchelier was really fascinated to see what my feet were like without the pointe shoes. I would wrap up each toe to protect them when I had a full day's work *en pointe*. The pointe shoe does a wonderful job of disguising the work and pain your feet go through. Creating the perfect line in your pointe shoes is one of the most important skills of a classical dancer.

Photos by Patrick Demarchelier/Hearst Communications Inc.

Chiffon Inspiring Juliet
APRIL 1993

With all the different styles we tried, it became a
very long day of shooting. The designer dresses
must have cost thousands, they certainly felt like
they did. Some of the clothes reminded me of the
roles I danced, so I naturally emulated the relevant
choreography for Patrick. I particularly remember
the concrete floor that I had to work on for the
whole day. There weren't many photos that didn't
have me dancing, so I was exhausted by the end.

*Photo by Patrick Demarchelier/Hearst
Communications Inc.*

4

SHIFTING THE BARRE

MADAME TUSSAUDS™

THE ALBERT MEMORIAL

THE MS AZURA – P&O CRUISE LINER

MADAME TUSSAUDS

To anyone growing up in London as I did, Madame Tussauds is one of those places we all know of, so to be invited to have a waxwork statue made of you is a big deal. It was certainly one of the more unusual experiences of my career. Many of the figures, historical or political, pop stars or members of the Royal Family, are depicted in a static upright or sitting posture. I was very pleased that my waxwork was going to appear in costume and in a balletic pose, celebrating my life as a ballet dancer.

Like the skaters Jayne Torvill and Christopher Dean, who are depicted in the movement and costumes of their memorable ice dance to Ravel's *Bolero*, for which they won gold at the 1984 Olympics in Sarajevo, I was going to appear 'in action' too. But what I hadn't fully appreciated beforehand was just how skilled and time-consuming a task it would be to realise this, with all the extraordinary attention to detail. It's not something that can just be done from photographs. We needed to decide what might be the best, most iconic ballet to represent. Working all this out was tricky. Of all the wonderful choices, we decided on *The Sleeping Beauty*, because it is not only such a classic ballet but also because founder Dame Ninette de Valois chose *The Sleeping Beauty* for the The Royal Ballet Company's first tour of the US, which was so well received after World War II.

When I was approached to model for the waxwork, I had just been performing in Sir Anthony Dowell's production, so I knew immediately which position would best identify with it. I chose the balancing *attitude derrière* from the Rose Adagio sequence in Marius Petipa's original choreography where Princess Aurora meets her four suitors. Technically it's a very tricky sequence in the ballet, where the princess greets each prince in turn, balancing *en pointe*, with the other leg raised behind in *attitude derrière*. It's that momentary point of balance, with the arms in fifth position, which is held steady in each of the greetings.

It was very important that the sculptor understood where the weight of the body is centred in this position, neither too far forward nor too far back but in the correct position, otherwise the final pose would just look wrong, out of balance and not to the classical ballet form (being very picky!). Because of this, I had to be photographed over and over from different angles, while in the pose, so they had all the references needed to be sure of getting the balance of the position right. There also had to be a sense of impending movement, as if the body was moving through a dance sequence, rather than just static.

Every aspect of my body, from the distance of my elbow to my wrist, the length of my thigh, the space between my mouth and my chin, for example, had to be measured and photographed for reference. The only parts of my body to be cast were my hands and feet. My feet had to be cast in my pointe shoes, and in the position they would be in the finished sculpture. That was difficult because a foot carrying the full weight of your body has a very specific position. So for this I had to stand *en pointe* in a bucket of alginate to create the impression from which the mould would be taken. After that, I had to dip my other foot into another bucket

Launch of Waxwork
8TH JULY 1997
Madame Tussauds, London

—

Photo by Peter Jordan/PA Images

of alginate, but this time in *its* correct position as if raised behind me. My hands also had to be as if they were elevated above my head in fifth position, again dipped in a bucket.

Not only did they cast my hands and feet, but also my teeth! My face was sculpted but then we had to match my eyes, which they did by going through trays and trays of glass eye balls, holding each against my own until they found the exact match for my kind of khaki-ish, hazel green eyes. Of course my hair, too, had to be a matched.

The model of my body wasn't made out of wax though, but was a 3D fibreglass mould. A specially made (and very expensive) Princess Aurora tutu was commissioned from the Royal Opera House costume department. It had to be made to fit the sculptured body – making it difficult to get on – because unlike a living body that can move and wriggle into a costume, this body couldn't! The beautiful tiara was also an original from the Royal Opera House team. I had just presumed they were going to have one of my old tutus and headdresses.

I can't remember how many trips I made to the studio near Acton in West London, at least 20 if not more, and after a long day's rehearsals I often found standing for the sculptor quite exhausting. On the 8th July 1997 I was finally unveiled at Madame Tussauds. To be honest, it was really odd to see this effigy of myself, the skin so pale and slightly transparent as it might look under stage lights. One difference was that the face wasn't in full stage makeup. Because stage makeup is designed to over-accentuate your features, close up it can look much too exaggerated and garish, so the makeup on the model is more understated.

My waxwork had been elevated onto a pedestal, so I had to stand on a box to be photographed next to it. To the public it was a slightly odd view, as you were effectively looking up my skirt into the different layers of net of the tutu. As a consequence, lots of people *kindly* sent me photos showing just that!

I did ask what would happen to it once I had retired as a dancer and they said, 'Oh, well the wax is just melted down and reused', which was an awful thought given all of their incredibly hard work! I wondered, couldn't I have it, perhaps? I could put it in a shed in the garden. But I believe that the waxwork of me still exists, which I was very happy to hear. Quite recently it was on display at the Madame Tussauds in Blackpool, when we were making an episode of *Strictly Come Dancing* there.

Launch of Waxwork
8TH JULY 1997
Madame Tussauds, London

Photo by Peter Jordan/PA Images

In Motion

DECEMBER 2016

These photos are stills from a documentary by
the BBC on my career. Here I am in the role of
Nikiya in *La Bayadère*, Act 1, with my partner,
the famous Kirov Theatre dancer, Igor Zelinsky.

Photos by Stephen Vaughan/BBC

THE ALBERT MEMORIAL

Being a West Londoner, I have passed the Albert Memorial regularly for nearly all of my life. As a young child I used to picnic by it and I have taken my own children there many times and I've always admired it, even if scootering around it at a mad pace!

Built in memory of Prince Albert after he died in 1861 aged just 42, the memorial was opened in 1872. By the late 1990s however, it was in very bad repair and in need of complete restoration. This was undertaken by English Heritage and included the stunning re-gilding of Prince Albert and the four angels at the very top just beneath the cross where I was photographed. The monument was under heavy scaffolding for a long time during its renovation, but the shoot was a last-minute idea, it wasn't planned. Someone realised that the scaffolding was coming down the very next day and what an opportunity it would be to create an image in such an iconic spot. This photo became part of the promotion for London Fashion Week 1998, as well as promoting the memorial's unveiling.

Photographer Laurie Lewis, who had photographed me a lot as a dancer, was commissioned for the shoot and I was going to wear a glorious, red couture gown by Neil Cunningham. I've always loved Neil's designs, which draw from the beautifully cut but simple 1950s style immortalised by actresses like Audrey Hepburn. He had made my silk organza wedding dress the previous year.

The shoot was at such short notice I did my own makeup and hair on the day and then, for safety reasons, I had to wear a hard hat, which I was afraid would ruin my French pleat. What's more, we hadn't the space to take anything as useful as a makeup bag or hairbrush up with us, and it was quite windy that day. So I was pretty worried about ending up with a wrinkled dress, dishevelled hair or smudged makeup after making it to the top.

The only way up was the via caged lift so Neil and I got to travel slowly up the memorial, past these beautiful gilded statues, the eight Virtues at the first level, then the first four angels and another four at the top, way above the canopy that covers the seated statue of Prince Albert. I hadn't realised how high it was – the memorial is 176 feet (54 m) tall! – and I became nervous that I might lose a shoe, it might slip off and fall down inside the canopy and hit Albert on the head, or something like that. The scaffolding moved ever so slightly as we shuffled around the platform, plus you could see all the way down to the ground. All this was a bit unnerving and didn't feel particularly safe, although we were assured that we were!

How amazing, though, to be so close to these pristine, perfectly gilded angels and to know that we were only a few of the handful of people who will ever see them up so close. They looked almost too perfect, because the gold leaf was so freshly applied. To create an image that would compliment the beauty and history of the monument, while dressed in this gorgeous couture gown and lying within the arms of a life-sized gold angel, was simply surreal. It was like being in a Renaissance painting.

The Albert Memorial
11TH MAY 1998

———

Photo by Laurie Lewis/Bridgeman Images

The Albert Memorial

11TH MAY 1998

Outside The Albert Memorial. I'm shown here
with the designer of this stunning red dress, Neil
Cunningham, and some craftsmen who are almost
at the end of the restoration work.

—————

Photo by Laurie Lewis/Bridgeman Images

The MS *Azura*

APRIL 2010

On the top deck of The MS *Azura* with the students of the lower school of The Royal Ballet. A few of these young men are now talented Principals in the Company.

———

Photo © P&O Cruises

THE MS AZURA – P&O CRUISE LINER

When a ship is named and launched, it's a longstanding naval tradition to appoint a Godmother to bring her good luck and protection, but I didn't know this until I received a letter out of the blue inviting me to be Godmother to the beautiful P&O cruise liner the MS *Azura*. What an honour! I discovered I was in very esteemed company because Dame Helen Mirren is Godmother to the *Azura's* sister ship, the MS *Ventura*.

For the launch event of the MS *Azura* in April 2010, I was asked to participate in a two-day event that would promote all the wonderful glamour and romance of a cruise ship. I was fortunate to have all my outfits designed by Jasper Conran, who I had worked with many times in the past. It was such a treat to be dressed by him.

The *Azura* has three magnificent dance floors, so a dance-themed celebration was definitely a good way to help launch the ship. We put together a sequence of live dance to be part of the naming ceremony. I worked on this with Kim Gavin, the choreographer with whom I would go on to collaborate on the BBC documentary *Darcey Bussell Dances Hollywood* in 2011 and the Olympics closing ceremony in 2012, to create something really memorable for the ship's launch.

We recreated routines from dance films such as Fred Astaire in *Follow the Fleet* (danced by The Royal Ballet junior school) and Elvis Presley in *Jailhouse Rock*; plus pieces of tango and jive, to showcase numerous different genres of dance. The last dance sequence I pre-recorded especially for the evening, the dramatic Fred Astaire and Cyd Charisse duet in *Bandwagon*.

I found out there's quite a lot of superstition around the naming of a ship, so I didn't take my role as Godmother to the *Azura* lightly. In fact, I rather felt the weight of it on my shoulders. So many people had worked so hard and taken so much pride in constructing a magnificent ship like this, you don't want to muck it up on the day. I think there were five – yes, five! – rehearsals of the naming ceremony. Luckily the bottle smashed and everything went to plan, complete with a spectacular fireworks display over the harbour at Southampton. Once the formalities were all over, we celebrated for the rest of the night with all the other guests and crew, dancing with everyone until the small hours. My daughters Phoebe and Zoe, then aged eight and six, also attended and had a wonderful time, not least because everyone made a huge fuss over them. They had such a good time that one of them asked delightfully, when I'm not around (i.e. dead!), do they get to inherit the role as Goddaughters?!

As a note to my daughters, I will be the official and very proud Godmother for *all* of MS *Azura's* seagoing life, until it's taken out of service. A year later my husband, daughters and I cruised the Norwegian fjords on it, which was a fabulous trip, with many of the crew kindly remembering us from the launch.

The Red Dress
APRIL 2010

Dancing with my fellow Royal Ballet dancer
Gary Avis at the evening naming ceremony of
The MS *Azura*. The full circle of the dress was
a joy to move in, designed by Jasper Conran.

Photo © P&O Cruises

Bottle Smashes
APRIL 2010

Opposite, I'm on the quay with a *very* heavy bottle of Champagne.

The photo above shows 'Take 1' in order to launch the Champagne bottle against the ship. I remember feeling quite a lot of pressure to get this done in one, and fortunately the ribbon cut and the champagne smashed successfully. No take two required.

Photos by © P&O Cruises

5

OFF POINTE

VIVA LA DIVA

DARCEY BUSSELL
DANCES HOLLYWOOD

VIVA LA DIVA

Viva la Diva was my first professional step away from the classical ballet world after I retired in 2007. I knew I'd find leaving The Royal Ballet difficult, that I'd miss my colleagues, the performing and the day-to-day involvement that comes from being part of a Company that I love. So I was very glad to have this distraction, a new show to develop and work on, despite my plans to leave for Australia with my family just six months later.

My manager, Steven Howard's prime expertise is in music and staging shows so he suggested, after I'd met Katherine Jenkins' manager Brian Lane, that Katherine and I create a show together. When we met, Katherine and I clicked. Our mutual love for the golden age of Hollywood musicals was clear. The ideas we had for a show immediately started to fly – effectively we were going to create a music and dance show based on these old musicals, which would see us combining our respective talents both separately and together. I was really excited by the idea us both singing and dancing. Yes, I sang a little too – which pushed me way out of my comfort zone, and was slightly (!) contrasted by Katherine's amazing voice.

Kim Gavin was creative director and producer and worked with us to create and choreograph all the routines for a two-hour show. After endless happy conversations, exchanging a hundred and one ideas, we put together a show inspired by the divas that inspired us – Judy Garland, Audrey Hepburn, Cyd Charisse, Barbra Streisand, Doris Day, Marilyn Monroe and many more. That is how the title for the show, *Viva la Diva*, emerged; its name just sort of suggested itself.

We included a mix of some big show-stopping numbers like 'Hey, Big Spender' and 'Diamonds Are a Girl's Best Friend', alongside beautiful arias sung by Katherine from Bizet's *Carmen* and songs made famous by Doris Day and Edith Piaf. We also included an iconic dance routine from *The Red Shoes*, made famous by ballerina Moira Shearer and another from *Funny Face* made famous by Audrey Hepburn.

We were spoilt for choice with so much wonderful material and struggled to limit our ideas but, despite this, I did ask Kenneth MacMillan's wife Deborah for permission to use his choreography from *Romeo and Juliet*, and also a *pas de deux* from his ballet, *Elite Syncopations*. My Royal Ballet ex-partners Jonathan Cope and Gary Avis came on-board for those and several other numbers.

Not only did I have to take singing lessons in preparation, I also had to brush up on my tap dancing, which I'd only studied for two years when I was really young. This was no hardship as I'm passionate about tap and I'm quite competitive, so when I knew I had to measure up to all the other tap dancers that had been doing it their whole working lives, I was really determined! There was also a flamenco routine that I absolutely loved, taught to us by the professional flamenco dancer and choreographer, Javier Marin. It was a challenge for me because it has a different rhythm to tap dancing, plus you have to learn how to push into the ground on the beat of the heels.

Viva la Diva
2008

A press photo promoting *Viva la Diva*, with Katherine Jenkins.

―――

Photo by Iris Brosch/John Parkinson Agency

Viva la Diva Rehearsal
2008

Rehearsing flamenco with choreographer
Javier Marin and Jonathan Cope.

Photos © Max Dodson 2008

I learnt such a lot about the demands and discipline required to change styles of dancing throughout this show, we danced tap, ballet, jazz, contemporary and Latin. In addition, some of the technical side was new to me, such as wearing an earpiece and microphone with a giant soundpack. What do you attach that to, when you're dancing?!

To end the show we did this huge Bob Fosse-inspired tap dancing number, which was so exhilarating it really took my breath away. In addition to a fabulous live band, some of the music was composed especially for the show, including the theme tune that was written for us by Gary Barlow. We were fortunate to have a successful 17-date, sell-out tour around the UK, including large venues like the O2 Arena in London.

Being involved in all aspects of the show, from conception through to its curtain call was wonderful. In spite of all the hard work and even though my body literally ached at the end of every show from all the chopping and changing of dance genres, it was so stimulating and energising. Thank you Katherine, thank you Kim and thank you to everyone involved for producing such a great show and for helping to take me into a completely new artistic space.

Viva la Diva Rehearsal
2008

Rehearsing in The Dance Attic studios in Fulham
Broadway, with flamenco choreographer Javier
Marin and Jonathan Cope. The photos show my
frustration as I try to pick up the difficult rhythms.

Photos © Max Dodson 2008

Viva la Diva Performance
2008

The photo opposite shows the tap dancing
sequence from the finale of *Viva la Diva* with
the full cast, which I absolutely loved performing.

Above is an image from the scene recreating
Bob Fosse-inspired choreography.

Photos © Tanya Chalkin 2008

DARCEY BUSSELL DANCES HOLLYWOOD

Ever since I can remember, I've loved the old Hollywood dance musicals. I grew up watching these films and they inspired me to become a dancer. Fred Astaire in *Top Hat* and *Blue Skies*, Gene Kelly in *Singin' in the Rain*, all those old favourites; the wonderful tunes and dance routines with their romance, wit and lyricism. So when I was invited to make a BBC documentary about these Hollywood musicals, I was delighted.

Initially I had thought the producers just wanted me to talk about the original shows, to interview other people and present the programme, but it turned out that they actually wanted me to dance some of these iconic numbers. The idea was to explore and emulate the talent of the original choreography and to replicate the precision, timing and discipline of these great dancers. Without the original choreographers around, however, we were going to have to recreate the routines from the filmed versions and to try to get them as exact as possible in order to do them justice. Working on the documentary was my friend Kim Gavin, an ex Royal Ballet dancer and one of the UK's leading creative directors, so he was in charge of the choreography, while conductor John Wilson was working on the orchestration of the musical scores from the films.

Given my love of these classic musicals and because I'd often dreamt how wonderful it would be to dance the original choreography, it was going to be such an exciting documentary to make.

But there was a catch. Several, in fact. Not only was I living in Australia, but I'd also injured my knee. Since we'd moved to Sydney in 2007 I'd been supporting the Sydney Dance Company and I used to do their classes. During a class in 2010 I'd managed to dislocate my knee and snap my anterior cruciate ligament, the ACL, which needed surgical repair. The time to recover fully from both the injury and the surgery is usually around eight months to a year. If I was going to do the dancing for this documentary, I would need to be back at a working level of fitness just five months after the operation. Even though I'd had two ankle surgeries in the past and I knew how to rehabilitate the joint (strengthening the muscles while the ligaments heal), I also knew that with a major joint like my knee it would take time. I was very anxious about it all.

I was going to dance four numbers: the Fred Astaire tap dancing role in 'Puttin' on the Ritz' from *Blue Skies*, Ginger Rogers' role dancing the foxtrot in 'Cheek to Cheek' from *Top Hat*, plus another number from *The Band Wagon* and, probably the most immediately memorable, the 'Good Morning' routine from *Singin' in the Rain*. Here I would be dancing Debbie Reynolds' role, alongside Australian dancers Steven Grace and Nathan Clarke, who were recreating the roles danced by Gene Kelly and Donald O'Connor. Only in the jazz piece from *The Band Wagon* (released in 1953, where Fred Astaire dances with Cyd Charisse) did we decide to do something different; Kim re-choreographed the piece to show how well it travelled into the 21st century, whilst keeping a lot of the original moves.

Cheek to Cheek
2011

Dancing with Nathan Clarke for a BBC documentary called *Darcey Bussell Dances Hollywood*. The opportunity to emulate any of this choreography was a dream.

Photo by Ross MacGibbon

So here I was, three years since I'd retired from fulltime dancing, five months after an operation on my knee, embarking on a physically demanding series of dance routines. I wondered how I was going to manage because I really wanted to do justice to the routines that I admired so much, and give it my absolutely best shot.

The biggest challenge of the four was going to be the tap dancing in 'Puttin' on the Ritz'. Fred would have rehearsed for about three months before he filmed it and due to modern documentary making I had four weeks! There was so much to think about, the timing had to be so exact and, of course, Fred had so much natural flair and musicality he made it look so easy.

I had done a bit of tap when I was about 11 or 12 years old, before switching fulltime to ballet and I had also done some tap in 2007/08 for the *Viva la Diva* show with Katherine Jenkins. But this was tap dancing in a different league! I went to a lot of classes and fortunately Nathan, with whom I danced every piece, is a very skilled tap dancer and he helped me enormously.

At the end of rehearsals every day, my knee was swollen and I was really concerned it wouldn't last the distance. It felt all right but it was always swollen, although I realised that in fact the tap dancing wasn't too strenuous on the knee. Whilst physically quite heavy-going with all the stamping, at least my leg was relatively parallel with my foot, unlike the turn out needed when twisting, jumping and pirouetting in ballet. So I just kept pummeling through the rhythms and tried not to feel too daunted by what I'd undertaken. I had to use every minute of studio time to rehearse and rehearse and it was essential that I didn't mark any of the moves before we filmed it.

When it came to the filming day of 'Puttin' on the Ritz', I was very aware that this was an iconic piece of choreography and here I was, a female dancer trying to emulate Fred Astaire and trying to tap dance in a top hat and tails and holding a cane. I wasn't fit enough to get through the whole routine in one go and I was sweating a lot in full costume and being under the studio lights didn't help. I felt the pressure and it was probably the hardest day of filming that I have ever experienced. It took several takes but I think we at least managed to capture the essence of this iconic piece.

'Cheek to Cheek,' the famous foxtrot danced in *Top Hat*, was a different matter altogether. Here Nathan and I were really trying to capture the feeling between Fred and Ginger. We copied the choreography exactly to emulate the film. The choreography was so beautiful, I really loved it, and the beautiful white feathered dress I wore as Ginger Rogers had almost as many feathers as her famous dress. I also got to interview some wonderful people who'd been involved with some of these productions: dance critics, other choreographers, designers and directors, and also Fred Astaire's daughter Ava and Gene Kelly's daughter Kerry, who was on set when they filmed *Singin' in the Rain*.

While it was like a dream come true, making this documentary was hard work, but we did it and my sincere thanks go to Kim Gavin, Steven Grace, Nathan Clarke, John Wilson and the directors Michael Waldman and Ross MacGibbon, plus everyone else who contributed, from Matthew Bourne to Bruce Oldfield. These photographs commemorate a dance documentary of which I am very proud and it was shown on Christmas Day in 2011.

Putting on the Ritz
2011

Playing Fred Astaire has been one of the most difficult things I have ever done.

Photos by Ross MacGibbon

Working the Hair
2011

We had to get the hair just right for me
to play Ginger Rogers.

Photo by Ross MacGibbon

The Famous Partnership

2011

These photos show Nathan Clarke and me recreating the famous partnership of Fred and Ginger.

Photos by Ross MacGibbon

'Cheek to Cheek', Take 50

2011

This dance had to be rehearsed over and over again
for the cameras, until we were satisfied that we had
captured the true feel of the era.

Photos by Ross MacGibbon

Good Morning!

2011

Dancing with Nathan Clarke and Stephen Grace.
This is a recreation of the famous scene from
Singin' in the Rain. I'm playing Debbie Reynolds,
Nathan is playing Gene Kelly and Stephen is
playing Donald O'Connor.

Photos by Ross MacGibbon

6

TO BE CONTINUED

OLYMPICS 2012 CLOSING CEREMONY

STRICTLY COME DANCING

OLYMPICS 2012 CLOSING CEREMONY

I had been retired from The Royal Ballet for five years and living with my family in Australia when I was approached by Kim Gavin, now creative director for the 2012 Summer Olympics closing ceremony, to ask if I would consider dancing for this event.

I was totally out of practice. I hadn't danced *en pointe* for about four years, which is not something you just get up and do again easily. I remember thinking I'll need to get myself back to classical ballet fitness to be able to dance a decent *pas de deux*, and it would take some time to get back to that but also to get my confidence back. And did I want to be seen again as a ballerina?

Still, it was such a huge honour to be asked and I had six or seven months to get ready, so I said yes, and immediately signed up for a daily ballet class to prepare. It was estimated that the worldwide audience was to be 750 million, with a British TV audience averaging over 20 million viewers, so I certainly felt that the pressure was on making a comeback live on television!

The Spirit of the Flame segment was to appear at the end of the ceremony, before the Olympic flame – from the beautiful cauldron designed by Thomas Heatherwick – was extinguished. My role was to embody the Spirit of the Flame, like a phoenix rising from the ashes, in a completely new piece of dance choreographed by Christopher Wheeldon and Alastair Marriott, with music composed by David Arnold. I would dance with four male dancers Ed Watson, Nehemiah Kish, Jonathan Cope and Gary Avis, and a 200-strong ensemble of the most enthusiastic dancers from many different British dance organisations.

There was quite a lot to work out in its staging, to make this work in the 80,000 capacity Olympic arena. While the 200 dancers were being rehearsed separately, Ed, Nehemiah, Jonathan and Gary had to find time in their busy schedules to rehearse secretly with me, mostly in a very unglamorous parking lot in Dagenham as it turned out. So, for the short time I was over from Australia prior to the event, that was an extra logistical difficulty.

Then I was told that for dramatic effect, I would be flown in from the top of the stadium (63 m/ 206 ft high) on a phoenix-shaped rig to begin the dance, just after the cauldron flames were lowered prior to being extinguished. What a great idea, I thought initially, but then it hit me... that's high! Now although I've done many physically challenging things over the years and I'm pretty fearless, I'm really not great with heights. The first time I climbed up with the rigging guys to see how it would work, I knew this was going to be something I'd need to get my head around prior to the performance on the night. But this was going to be such a one-off experience that I decided I would go for it.

I also had great faith in the experts building the 'baby phoenix' on which I was to fly into the arena. The Total Solutions Group were producing a lot of the structures for the ceremony and I visited their workrooms to see the winged metal structure to which I'd be strapped, that would then be suspended by two wires for the flight. We also had to work out how much movement might occur as I flew through the air, with only a small footplate on which to stand and with my straps holding me securely in place. Before my first attempt, I watched as they tested it with another girl in the harness, which was really helpful. I could see how it worked, see her confidence in how safe it was and what was going to happen.

The first time I gave it a go, it took about 15 minutes to climb up to the top of the stadium and it was quite a windy and wet day. I remember thinking, 'If it's like this on the night, I'm going to look less like a Spirit of the Flame and more like a drowned rat when I appear.' The second time was around 2 am in the empty stadium, but it was useful to do it at night and get a sense of what the performance might be like. I was anxious about the timing because I had to hit the stage and start the choreography on a musical cue, and that meant getting out of the quick-release belt (the only thing holding me fast) that was around my waist, and off the rig smoothly. As this was a complete one-off there had to be no mistakes, because if you miss your cue and don't start well, it can affect the whole performance from beginning to end. I also didn't practice with the fireworks shooting out behind me, they were reserved for the performance which was the third and final time I made that descent.

On the actual night of the ceremony, I got up to the top of the arena in good time, about 45 minutes early-wrapped in my ski outfit to keep warm. It was really the strangest place to do a ballet barre! I had one of the best views of the whole ceremony and looking down on it before participating was quite extraordinary.

The crew got me rigged up very early so I was hanging out over the stadium for the whole of Take That's performance. Listening to Gary Barlow, Mark Owen and Howard Donald sing *Rule the World* from that height was rather wonderful and got me into the mood as I swayed above them. While the weather on the night was fine I was wearing only a thin Lycra one-piece, but I realised I needn't have worried about getting cold and my muscles stiffening up while I waited, because I was hanging straight over the cauldron's flames, its heat was keeping me very warm.

Suddenly the moment arrived, the rig was released and with the fireworks blazing behind my feet, I set off flying across the stadium. It was an extraordinary combination of being free but focused, mixed with adrenalin and anticipation. To make sure I descended on time, the rig was speeded up a little. I landed with a bit of a bump, which was edited out for transmission on the time lapse. There were two dancers waiting to hold the structure as I released the safety strap and ran into the centre for my first lift, in time to hit the beat on a crescendo of music that heralded the start of our part of the performance – my focus was just to get all the placing perfect for my four male dancers. It was so strange to be dancing on a round, with no official front to the stage and in strong lights that we had not experienced before. But it all came together well, in spite of the responsibility I'd felt in playing the role of The Spirit of the flame.

The closing ceremony was such a phenomenal event to be involved with. I felt so privileged to have been a part of it, with all the thousands of sports men and women within the gigantic Union Jack stage. I've danced for the Queen and at other significant events and galas, but nothing quite like this. It was really, really special and an experience I'll remember and treasure forever. I'm so glad they asked me, and I'm so glad I said yes.

In Planning
2012

Behind-the-scenes planning for my costume and steel wings, which I would use to fly from the top of the arena to the middle of the Olympic stadium.

———

Photos by Steven Howard

The Team

2012

These photos on the left and above show the hard working team behind the incredible vision of Kim Gavin, director and producer of the closing ceremony.

The photos on the right show my dancing men: Ed Watson, Nehmiah Kish, Jonathan Cope and Gary Avis. The last photo is of the choreographers, Allistair Marriot, Jonathan Howles and Christopher Wheeldon.

Photos by Steven Howard

The Dress Rehearsal
2012

The series of rehearsals were touch and go...
from beginning to end! But it all worked on
the night.

———

Photos by Steven Howard

The Olympic Flame
2012

In my role as the phoenix I was to put out the
Olympic Flame. I was incredibly honoured to
be chosen to finish the closing ceremony.

Photo by Saeed Khan/AFP/Getty Images

STRICTLY COME DANCING

It was announced in April 2012 that I would be joining the *Strictly Come Dancing* judging team, alongside Len Goodman, Bruno Tonioli and Craig Revel Horwood. I was absolutely thrilled about this, and a little terrified. Alesha Dixon (who won series five of the show in 2007) had decided to leave *Strictly* after being a judge for three years up until 2011.

I had first appeared on *Strictly* as a guest, when I danced a piece from *Viva la Diva* with Katherine Jenkins and I had appeared again as a guest judge in 2009, but of course I hadn't known then that I would later be invited to return as a judge fulltime. Joining the team for the programme's eleventh series was very different to guest judging. Previously, I had literally 'dropped in' to do the filming and give my professional critique. I didn't really have the chance to get to know the other judges, for example, so this was going to be a totally different experience.

Prior to the new season, we had to film a trailer to promote the show, and these photographs were taken from the preparation for that. The producers wanted to raise the awareness that I was joining the show and that I had been a professional dancer all my life. We filmed in a grand house in South London in a large, dramatic room with a wonderful fireplace, candelabras and drapes, which had been dressed up to look very bling-y and 'Strictlyfied'.

The day of filming the trailer was surreal. I had loved the show and been watching it for years and years and now I was about to be one of the fulltime judges. Also, none of the judges knew exactly what we were going to do on the day, except for possibly Craig! There had been no rehearsals to prepare for it, which was unusual. Alongside the four of us judges were professional dancers Ian Waite, who I already knew, and Natalie Lowe. The plan was revealed: the three male judges were to be filmed doing a dance turn with me. None of us had been specifically told about the dancing and there was some consternation, from Len in particular. Coming together for the first time as a new team, everybody was obviously a bit nervous, but as we worked out what was wanted of us and what we had to dance, I didn't feel too out of my depth or too much the 'new girl' because we were all having to work it out together, there and then, which really helped us bond.

With Ian and Natalie helping to choreograph, suddenly I was doing a little tango with Len, then having to execute a swivel, turn and full backbend with Bruno and then a drag and multiple turns with Craig, making sure we finished in time with the music. All of which made it a real ice breaker and a very immediate way to get to know them! Afterwards, all the dance sequences were linked and edited together to create the trailer.

The dress I'm wearing was specially made for this day and I had already been for a number of fittings with the lovely designers. The idea was that the dress would mirror the famous *Strictly Come Dancing* glitter ball (and winner's trophy) that appears in the opening credits. So it had pieces of glass attached to the material. That made it very beautiful but really quite heavy. Another problem

Meeting the Judges
AUGUST 2012

The making of the advertisement announcing my first appearance as a new judge on *Strictly Come Dancing*, and meeting my new best mates, Len Goodman, Bruno Tonioli and Craig Revel Horwood!

———

Photo by James Robinson

was that the pieces of glass were scratchy, so I had to take care when I swept my arms past my body, but I still ended up with scratches all over my arms after dancing in it all day! Sadly, I couldn't keep the dress, because it was very special, and it went back into the costume department. My shoes were actually from Zara, and had been embellished by the costume department to match the dress.

There was also a long, dark purple hooded cape made for me to wear over the top, making me a look a bit like the woman in the Scottish Widows advertisements. Initially I was to come down the stairs, my identity hidden, then twirl the cloak, lower my hood and reveal myself. But fortunately we didn't do this.

To be honest, I was naïve as to all the build up about me coming onto the show. Having only just arrived back from living in Australia, I had thought it would be rather more low-key with maybe just a press release in the newspapers the week before! But I couldn't have been more wrong. It was tremendously exciting to join *Strictly Come Dancing* in 2012 and it felt like a very natural progression, sharing my expertise and love of dance.

These days, I always look forward to seeing the progress the celebrities make and think what a privilege it is for them to have one-on-one sessions every day with a professional dancer. They work hard, learn a lot in a short time and have an experience they will never forget. The teamwork, choreography, expertise and commitment that goes into *Strictly* week after week, is outstanding. It is such a positive programme to be a part of: I love it.

Commercial Preparations
2012

My dress in these photos (above) was designed
to resemble the mirrored glitter ball that is the icon
of *Strictly Come Dancing*. The lovely makeup artist
Gina Kneiffel is shown (opposite) getting me ready.

Photos by James Robinson

Dancing Behind the Scenes

2012

In the photo below, I'm dancing with Craig
Revel Horwood.

On the right, with Len Goodman and Bruno
Tonioli in the famous Blackpool Tower
Ballroom. Dress designed by Stuart Parvin.

—

Photos by Guy Levy

The New LADY Judge

<small>28TH AUGUST 2017</small>

The very welcome arrival of Shirley Ballas to the *Strictly* family, who took over as head judge after Len Goodman stepped down.

———

Photo by Gareth Cattermole/Getty Images

Strictly on Tour
2018

My first tour with *Strictly Come Dancing*, back stage
at The Arena Birmingham. It brought back all the
memories of being on tour during my dance career.
Their energy never flagged for the whole of the
tour – extraordinary.

Photo courtesy of the Darcey Bussell Collection

Strictly Christmas Special
2014

Photo by Guy Levy/BBC

Rumba and Jive

Dancing with the gorgeous Ian Waite in a jive (2009) and a rumba (2012). No pressure being on the famous *Strictly* dance floor.

Photo by Guy Levy/BBC

Mandarin Oriental Campaign
2006
Margot Fonteyn studio, Covent Garden

When you come to the end of any important
photo shoot it's nice to let off steam… and Mary
was happy to have a laugh too! There are always
famous images that you can't help but replicate
in jest, the right-hand picture is me pretending
to be Fiona Butler on the tennis court in 1976.

Photos © Mary McCartney

Becoming a Dame
MAY 2018

It was the most beautiful day when my husband, daughters and I went to Buckingham Palace for my investiture. We were a little late (just for the rehearsal, not the investiture ceremony itself) as the Mall was closed to cars, so we had to dash across Green Park and then battle our way through the crowds. On the day, it was so exciting to be standing behind Sir Paul McCartney in the queue and such an honour to be given my DBE from Her Majesty the Queen herself. When I was being photographed by the press afterwards I dropped my beautiful medal and was very worried that I would be photographed picking it up from the gravel… but I was rescued by the delightful Yeomen of the guard !

Photos by Angus Forbes

Adorned

APRIL 2018

Getting increasingly creative in my old age.
The designer Harvey Brown layers the eccentric
objects and bugs over the clean photograph of
the muse. Fabulously theatrical, quirky, humorous
and very original.

———

*Photos by David Scheinmann/designed by
Harvey Brown*

PHOTO CREDITS

Front Cover   Mark Abrahams/Trunk Archive
Back Cover   Asya Verzhbinsky/ArenaPal

129 Laurie Lewis/Bridgeman Images
130 © P&O Cruises
132 © P&O Cruises
133 © P&O Cruises
134 © P&O Cruises
135 © P&O Cruises

138 Iris Brosch/John Parkinson Agency
140 © Max Dodson 2008
141 © Max Dodson 2008
142 © Max Dodson 2008
143 © Max Dodson 2008
144 © Tanya Chalkin 2008
145 © Tanya Chalkin 2008
146 Ross MacGibbon
149 Ross MacGibbon
150 Ross MacGibbon
152 Ross MacGibbon
153 Ross MacGibbon
154 Ross MacGibbon
155 Ross MacGibbon
156 Ross MacGibbon
157 Ross MacGibbon

160 Carl Court/AFP/Getty Images
163 Steven Howard
164 Steven Howard
165 Steven Howard
166 Steven Howard
167 Steven Howard
169 Saeed Khan/AFP/Getty Images
171 James Robinson
172 James Robinson
173 James Robinson
174 Guy Levy/BBC
175 Guy Levy/BBC
176 Gareth Cattermole/Getty Images
177 Courtesy of the Darcey Bussell Collection
178 Guy Levy/BBC
179 Guy Levy/BBC
180 © Mary McCartney
181 © Mary McCartney
182 Angus Forbes
183 Angus Forbes
184 David Scheinmann/designed by Harvey Brown
185 David Scheinmann/designed by Harvey Brown

189 Allen Jones

Allen Jones
1997
National Portrait Gallery, London

There were two paintings made in this style, both are almost life size; one hangs in the National Portrait Gallery and the other, pictured here, is held in a private collection.

Painting by Allen Jones

ACKNOWLEDGEMENTS

My sincere thanks to everyone involved with the making of *Darcey Bussell: Evolved*.

My old friend and colleague Janine Limberg is once again key to making a book like this and my most sincere thanks must go to her first. Present at nearly every shoot I ever did with The Royal Ballet, she remembers names and places (in her well kept diaries!) that sometimes I have, regretfully, forgotten.

For the second time, it has been a real pleasure working with the very professional team at Hardie Grant, led on this occasion by Stephen King. My thanks to my editor Molly Ahuja, who worked tirelessly and was very patient as I changed things, often in quite a drastic manner, the book's hard-working and talented designer Clare Skeats, Emma Marijewycz and the whole team.

Jasper Conran has been a long time friend and support to me, and I am so grateful for him agreeing to write the foreword to this book. He very kindly wrote that I was the only choice when in 1989 he wanted to do a shoot with a Royal Ballet dancer, well almost 30 years later, I felt the same way when thinking about who I would l like to write this foreword. I have always been a great admirer of his style and vision. Thank you so much Jasper.

Nothing would have materialised without the opportunities afforded to me by being part of The Royal Ballet and having that break of good fortune given to me by Sir Kenneth MacMillan. After ballet, the teams around me have been instrumental. My manager Steven Howard, the wonderful Carol Howard and miracle working Gina Kneiffel have created one of the most productive of working environments and we have great fun at the same time as working long hard hours. Thank you guys! Behind everything I do is the ever reliable and talented Charlotte Toosey, my friend and P.A. for almost 20 years, my thanks as always.

This book is all about collaboration with other artists and exposing their superb talent. I thank them all for their imagination and skill.

I would like to express my heartfelt thanks to the photographers whose work is featured in this book for their generosity and cooperation:

Anthony Crickmay, Mario Testino, Patrick Demarchelier, Laurie Lewis, Bill Cooper, Leslie E. Spatt, Allen Jones, Richard Avedon, Mary McCartney, Jimmy Wormser, Chris Nash, Clive Arrowsmith, John Stoddart, Arthur Elgort, John Swannell, Lord Anthony Snowdon, Annie Leibovitz, Herbie Knott, Glen Copus, David M. Bennett, Eric Richmond, Reg Wilson, Ken Towner, Nils Jorgensen, David Buckland, Sheila Rock, David Scheinmann, Andy Whale, Jason Bell, Tim Richmond, Iris Brosch, Max Dodson, Tanya Chalkin, Stephen Vaughan, Carl Court, Saeed Khan, James Robinson, Steven Howard, The Royal Ballet Collections, Audi, P&O Cruises and film Director Ross MacGibbon.